SPECTRUM®
Test Practice 8
With Free Online Resources for each U.S. State

Published by Spectrum®
an imprint of Carson-Dellosa Publishing LLC
Greensboro, NC

MW01131989

Spectrum®
An imprint of Carson-Dellosa Publishing LLC
P.O. Box 35665
Greensboro, NC 27425 USA

SPECTRUM TEST PRACTICE
Table of Contents
Grade 8

The Common Core State Standards

What Are the Standards?

The Common Core State Standards have been adopted by most U.S. states. They were developed by a state-led initiative to make sure all students are prepared for success in college and in the global, twenty-first century workforce. They provide a clear understanding of what students are expected to learn in English language arts and mathematics.

These new learning standards for your child are:

- Rigorous.

- Based on the best available evidence and research.

- Aligned with college and work expectations.

- Benchmarked to the highest educational standards from around the world.

What Do the English Language Arts Standards Mean for My Student?

In grade 8, English language arts standards focus on reading, writing, speaking and listening, and language skills (grammar and usage).

These standards set expectations for what it means to be a skilled reader and writer in the twenty-first century. They provide strategies for reading fiction and nonfiction closely and attentively. They help students look for evidence and make critical judgments about the vast amount of print and digital information available.

What Do the Mathematics Standards Mean for My Student?

Examples of grade 8 mathematics standards include functions (using functions to describe relationships between numbers) and geometry (understanding the Pythagorean Theorem).

These standards increase the depth and focus of math topics studied in each grade. Instead of sampling a wide variety of skills each year, students work to develop deep understanding and mastery of a few concepts.

Free Online State-Specific Test Practice

For additional **free** *Spectrum Test Practice* resources customized to your child's grade level and the U.S. state where you live, follow these instructions:

1. Go to:

   carsondellosa.com/spectrum

2. Click on *Spectrum Test Practice Free Online Materials* and register to download your free practice pages.

3. Download and print PDF pages customized for your state and your child's grade level.

Online Features Include:

- Links to Common Core State Standards information for your state

- A comprehensive practice test aligned to Common Core English language arts and mathematics standards for your child's grade level

- State-specific test items within the practice test, designated by this symbol: **1.**

  These items are aligned to the unique standards that have been adopted by your state in addition to Common Core State Standards.

- An answer key for practice test pages

How to Use This Book

Time spent practicing for standardized tests will benefit your child greatly. With the adoption of Common Core State Standards by most U.S. states, educators are relying more than ever on test results to compare your child's progress with that of others around the nation and the world. The resources in this book will help ease anxieties and prepare your child for test day.

What's Inside?

- **Lesson pages** contain sample questions and examples related to a specific skill. The assumption is that your student has received prior instruction on the topics. These pages can provide focused practice.

- **Sample tests** are shorter tests with questions about one subtopic.

- **Practice tests** are comprehensive tests with questions about the entire content area.

Practice Options

Choose how you will use the materials to meet the needs of your student.

- Select pages matching the skills your student needs to practice most.

- Assign lesson pages for practice throughout the week. End the week with a sample or practice test related to those skills.

- Administer a timed practice test in a quiet setting. For an eighth grade student, allow 1.17 minutes per question. After the test, check answers together and talk about what was most difficult.

Test-Taking Clues

- Look for the symbol shown above throughout the book. Talk about the clues with your child.

- Read and review directions and examples. Talk about how test questions look and point out words and phrases that often appear in directions.

- Skip difficult questions, returning to them if time allows.

- Guess at questions you do not know.

- Answer all the questions.

- Try to stay relaxed and approach the test with confidence!

READING: VOCABULARY

● Lesson 1: Synonyms

Directions: Read each question carefully. Fill in the circle of the word that means the same or about the same as the underlined word.

Examples

A. To be **feeble**
- (A) frail
- (B) notorious
- (C) strong
- (D) wrong

B. To be **petite**
- (F) lonely
- (G) small
- (H) uncertain
- (J) clever

 Clue If you are not sure which answer is correct, take your best guess. Eliminate answer choices you know are wrong.

● Practice

1. To **cherish**
- (A) distort
- (B) fool
- (C) adore ●
- (D) loathe

2. Something **antique**
- (F) dense
- (G) unpleasant
- (H) timid
- (J) old ●

3. An **opponent**
- (A) colleague ●
- (B) friend
- (C) foe
- (D) chum

4. Something **dense**
- (F) long
- (G) outside
- (H) thick ●
- (J) mountainous

5. To **commence**
- (A) close
- (B) start ●
- (C) fill
- (D) peddle

6. To **vault**
- (F) attempt ●
- (G) reply
- (H) answer
- (J) leap

7. To **respond**
- (A) answer ●
- (B) flex
- (C) correspond
- (D) dispute

8. To **request**
- (F) question
- (G) clean
- (H) ask ●
- (J) drag

STOP

READING: VOCABULARY

● Lesson 2: Antonyms

Directions: Read each item carefully. Fill in the circle that corresponds to the word that means the opposite of the underlined word.

Examples

A. <u>forbidden</u>
- (A) allowed
- (B) stolen
- (C) clean
- (D) prohibited

B. <u>brave</u>
- (F) courageous
- (G) afraid
- (H) lonely
- (J) tardy

Clue If you are not sure which answer is correct, take your best guess. Eliminate answer choices you know are wrong. Remember that you are choosing the opposite of the underlined word.

● Practice

1. <u>desolate</u>
   - (A) dry
   - (B) average
   - (C) desert
   - (D) crowded

2. <u>lanky</u>
   - (F) short
   - (G) tall
   - (H) stocky
   - (J) thin

3. <u>whisper</u>
   - (A) smell
   - (B) endure
   - (C) calm
   - (D) shout

4. <u>locate</u>
   - (F) pinpoint
   - (G) collapse
   - (H) lose
   - (J) find

5. <u>sorrow</u>
   - (A) joy
   - (B) sadness
   - (C) silly
   - (D) stoic

6. <u>peril</u>
   - (F) danger
   - (G) quiet
   - (H) safety
   - (J) malice

7. <u>peaceful</u>
   - (A) cowardly
   - (B) beautiful
   - (C) suspicious
   - (D) belligerent

8. <u>expensive</u>
   - (F) costly
   - (G) cheap
   - (H) pricey
   - (J) satisfying

STOP

Name _____ Date_____

READING: VOCABULARY

● **Lesson 3: Multi-Meaning Words**

Directions: Read each item carefully. Fill in the circle that corresponds to the answer that fits best in both sentences.

Examples

A. When will the bell ___ to end this class? Carmen received a ___ for Christmas.
- (A) ring
- (B) invitation
- (C) shirt
- (D) sound

B. The Congressman hired a new ___. A ___ is missing from the book.
- (F) summons
- (G) call
- (H) page
- (J) pass

Clue If you are not sure which answer is correct, make your best guess. Eliminate answer choices you know are wrong and choose the word that can be used in both sentences.

● **Practice**

1. Rake the ___ in the fall. Tommy ___the building.
- (A) ran
- (B) lawn
- (C) fired
- (D) leaves

2. The runner will ___ the mark. The athlete suffered a broken ___.
- (F) promise
- (G) toe
- (H) leave
- (J) erase

3. The animal fell into the ___. The game will ___the two best teams as opponents.
- (A) pit
- (B) hole
- (C) feature
- (D) crossfire

4. The carpenter had just the right ___. I should now ___ the bus.
- (F) slide
- (G) board
- (H) abandon
- (J) hammer

5. The tree grew a new ___. The new bank built a ___ facility outside the city.
- (A) trunk
- (B) leaf
- (C) building
- (D) branch

6. He was brought in as a relief ___. The ___ was filled with fresh water.
- (F) doctor
- (G) bottle
- (H) pitcher
- (J) general

STOP

READING: VOCABULARY

● Lesson 4: Words in Context

Directions: Read each sentence carefully. Look for a clue in each of the sentences that will help you to decide the word that will be the best choice to fill in the blank.

Examples

A. Pack ___ pairs of socks. You will need a fresh pair every day.

- (A) warm
- (B) numerous
- (C) clean
- (D) wool

B. A rich man gives. A ___ organization receives.

- (F) needy
- (G) unhealthy
- (H) common
- (J) professional

 Clue Skim each sentence. Use the meaning of what you read to find the right choice. If necessary, try substituting each answer choice in the blank.

● Practice

1. Because the knife was dull, I had to ___ the blade.
   - (A) burn
   - (B) carry
   - (C) sharpen
   - (D) roll

2. For lunch I had a slice of ___ and a roast beef sandwich.
   - (F) life
   - (G) haddock
   - (H) melon
   - (J) caution

3. I was ___ of my father's decision by telephone.
   - (A) refrained
   - (B) denied
   - (C) alarmed
   - (D) informed

4. Tom's family was most impressed with the ___ setting of the cabin in the forest.
   - (F) tranquil
   - (G) warlike
   - (H) everyday
   - (J) expensive

5. A stoplight was installed at the ___ of Grant and Columbus.
   - (A) rescinded
   - (B) intersection
   - (C) plantation
   - (D) painting

6. Samuel, the ___ of the family, paid for everyone's dinner.
   - (F) patrician
   - (G) patron
   - (H) partnership
   - (J) patriarch

READING: VOCABULARY

● Lesson 5: Words From Greek and Latin

Directions: Choose the best answer for each question.

Example

A. The Latin root *pac* means "peace." Which word means "to establish peace"?

- Ⓐ pachyderm
- Ⓑ pacify
- Ⓒ impact
- Ⓓ compact

● Practice

1. The Latin suffix *-fer* means "to carry." Which word means "to change from one to another"?
   - Ⓐ suffer
   - Ⓑ ferment
   - Ⓒ transfer
   - Ⓓ fertile

2. Which set of words contains the Greek suffix meaning "trait"?
   - Ⓕ heroism, optimism, witticism
   - Ⓖ discussion, profession, revision
   - Ⓗ mileage, storage, wreckage
   - Ⓙ barbarian, historian, musician

3. Which set of words contains the Latin prefix *pro-*, meaning "in favor of"?
   - Ⓐ profess, proofer, probe
   - Ⓑ proceed, progress, propulsion
   - Ⓒ probable, protein, problem
   - Ⓓ prom, proper, program

4. The Greek prefix *micro-* means "small." Which word means "a small amount of gravity"?
   - Ⓕ microgravity
   - Ⓖ microwave
   - Ⓗ microcapsule
   - Ⓙ microzero

5. Which word set contains the Latin root meaning "make"?
   - Ⓐ describe, inscribe, prescribe
   - Ⓑ bicycle, cycle, cyclone
   - Ⓒ unit, unite, unison
   - Ⓓ satisfaction, factory, manufacture

6. Which word set contains the Latin suffix *-able*, meaning "can be done"?
   - Ⓕ constable, table, tablet
   - Ⓖ ablest, ability, stability
   - Ⓗ changeable, laughable, readable
   - Ⓙ gullible, suitable, venerable

STOP

READING: VOCABULARY

● **Lesson 6: Shades of Meaning**

Directions: Choose the best answer for each question.

Examples

A. **Which sentence uses the underlined word most accurately?**

- (A) I boarded a <u>dinghy</u> to travel 3,000 miles <u>across</u> the ocean.
- (B) I boarded a <u>ship</u> to travel 3,000 miles across the ocean.
- (C) I boarded a <u>ferry</u> to travel 3,000 miles across the ocean.
- (D) I boarded a <u>speedboat</u> to travel 3,000 miles <u>across</u> the ocean.

B. **Which word best completes the sentence?**

Our teacher permitted us to dress _____ for the field trip.

- (F) casually
- (G) sloppily
- (H) carelessly
- (J) cheaply

● **Practice**

1. **Which analogy best describes the relationship between tool and user?**
   - (A) Plant is to harvest as cook is to eat.
   - (B) City is to state as state is to nation.
   - (C) Ear is to hear as eye is to see.
   - (D) Microscope is to biologist as telescope is to astronomer.

2. **When Mr. Nyung entered our noisy classroom, he said, "I can see you've been using this opportunity to work hard."**

   This sentence
   - (F) is a pun.
   - (G) personifies the classroom.
   - (H) is an example of verbal irony.
   - (J) symbolizes fear.

3. **Which set contains words that are not similar in meaning?**
   - (A) foster, create, facilitate, harbor
   - (B) participate, share, protect, partake
   - (C) punctual, timely, prompt, immediate
   - (D) home, dwelling, quarters, lodging

4. **Fertilizer is to soil as vitamins are to body.**

   This analogy shows a cause-and-effect relationship because
   - (F) both fertilizer and vitamins provide nourishment.
   - (G) neither soil nor bodies require fertilizer or vitamins.
   - (H) soil is not similar to vitamins.
   - (J) fertilizer is a substitute for vitamins.

GO ON

READING: VOCABULARY

● Lesson 6: Shades of Meaning (cont.)

5. After a long day of guarding the house, I am ready to eat dinner. I quiz my owner. She understands; a bowl of dog food appears before me. My question did not go unnoticed!

   The reader knows this is an example of personification because

   - (A) the dog is speaking in the first person.
   - (B) dogs sometimes quiz their owners.
   - (C) only dogs beg for food.
   - (D) the dog's point of view is exaggerated.

6. **Which word best completes the sentence?**

   Maria wanted a modest celebration, so she politely requested that any gifts be _____.

   - (F) premium
   - (G) affordable
   - (H) extravagant
   - (J) worn out

7. **Which does not contain a pun?**
   - (A) A reporter went to the new ice cream shop to get the scoop.
   - (B) This book about anti-gravity is impossible to put down.
   - (C) She is as happy as a pig in mud.
   - (D) That globe means the world to our social studies teacher.

8. If someone said, "What lovely weather we're having!" during a severe thunderstorm, you would recognize it as verbal irony because
   - (F) it is a twist on the word *lovely*.
   - (G) the speaker is making a comparison.
   - (H) the weather is actually unpleasant.
   - (J) lovely weather is common during severe thunderstorms.

9. **Which analogy describes a sequential relationship?**
   - (A) One is to first as three is to third.
   - (B) Ear is to hear as tongue is to mouth.
   - (C) Preface is to book as introduction is to speech.
   - (D) Goose is to geese as cow is to cattle.

10. **If your friend told you he was hungry enough to eat all the food in a grocery store, he would be using what figure of speech?**
    - (F) pun
    - (G) metaphor
    - (H) simile
    - (J) hyperbole

11. **An antonym for *churlish* is *polite*. So, a synonym for *churlish* would be**
    - (A) generous.
    - (B) rude.
    - (C) etiquette.
    - (D) unhappy.

Name _____   Date_____

READING: VOCABULARY
SAMPLE TEST

Directions: Read each item carefully.

Examples

For Example A, choose the word that correctly completes both sentences.	**For Example B, choose the word that means the opposite of the underlined word.**

A. Tim seems to have good ___. Birds can ___ a storm.

- (A) judgment
- (B) feel
- (C) sense
- (D) reasoning

B. <u>inevitable</u> situation

- (F) avoidable
- (G) confusing
- (H) stressful
- (J) enjoyable

For numbers 1–8, find the word or words that mean the same or almost the same as the underlined word.

1. <u>surprise</u> verdict
- (A) question
- (B) decision
- (C) unusual
- (D) investment

2. <u>somber</u> moment
- (F) passing
- (G) fleeting
- (H) bleak
- (J) joyful

3. <u>recollect</u> the past
- (A) forget
- (B) ignore
- (C) remember
- (D) separate

4. <u>plentiful</u> supply
- (F) abundant
- (G) scarce
- (H) fresh
- (J) rationed

5. <u>irritate</u> the teacher
- (A) accommodate
- (B) irk
- (C) pacify
- (D) moderate

6. <u>deter</u> others
- (F) encourage
- (G) follow
- (H) satisfy
- (J) discourage

7. <u>brief</u> statement
- (A) lengthy
- (B) concise
- (C) hollow
- (D) untrue

8. improper <u>behavior</u>
- (F) attitude
- (G) conduct
- (H) experience
- (J) useful

GO ON

READING: VOCABULARY
SAMPLE TEST (cont.)

For numbers 9–12, find the word that means the opposite of the underlined word.

9. **feel enmity**
   - (A) disappoint
   - (B) friendship
   - (C) impatience
   - (D) relief

10. **ignite a fire**
    - (F) extinguish
    - (G) observe
    - (H) light
    - (J) approach

11. **cancel the subscription**
    - (A) erase
    - (B) confirm
    - (C) eliminate
    - (D) hire

12. **deep despair**
    - (F) depression
    - (G) application
    - (H) maintenance
    - (J) optimism

For numbers 13–16, read each item and decide on the best choice for the blank space by using the clues in each statement.

13. **He keeps a ___ of candy in his locker.**
    - (A) locker
    - (B) hoard
    - (C) shelter
    - (D) racket

14. **A rich but ___ man.**
    - (F) humble
    - (G) wealthy
    - (H) poor
    - (J) prosperous

15. **Gold is a ___ metal.**
    - (A) canister
    - (B) rich
    - (C) hard
    - (D) precious

16. **The school uniform was the correct ___.**
    - (F) code
    - (G) attire
    - (H) response
    - (J) racket

For numbers 17–18, choose the word that correctly completes both sentences.

17. **The ___ led to their freedom from rule by England. The tire made one complete ___.**
    - (A) handsome
    - (B) insurance
    - (C) revolution
    - (D) talk

18. **Soup is cooking on the ___. Out west, cattle roam the open ___.**
    - (F) range
    - (G) prairie
    - (H) plains
    - (J) stove

READING: COMPREHENSION

● Lesson 7: Main Idea

Directions: Read each item carefully. Then choose the correct answer and the circle that corresponds to that choice.

Example

Tyler wanted a new cell phone to take with him to college. His father bought him one but told Tyler that he would have to pay for any extra minutes that were not included in the monthly charge.

A. **The message in the passage for Tyler is**

- (A) Buy the phone yourself.
- (B) Tell your friends not to call.
- (C) Keep track of the minutes that have been used each month.
- (D) Confusion is a big issue here.

● **Practice** **Clue** Skim the passage and then answer the questions. Refer back to the passage to find the answers. You don't have to reread the passage for each question.

A Childhood Promise

In a sandy cotton field in Georgia, a boy stood up. He looked at his bleeding hands. The cotton bolls had sliced his hands, but he wasn't thinking about the cuts. He was imagining different landscapes, like the ones his uncle had seen during his travels in the Navy. The boy promised himself that one day he would enlist in the Navy. He vowed that he would go to college, too, even though none of his family had ever attended college. That boy was James E. Carter, better known as Jimmy, and he would grow up to become president of the United States.

That boy achieved all he had set out to achieve, plus much he could not have imagined for himself. Through it all, he never forgot what it was like to live among desperately poor people. Instead of isolating himself from the poverty that had surrounded him as a child, he attacked the causes of poverty. Perhaps the example he provides is his greatest accomplishment.

1. **What is the main idea of this reading?**
   - (A) Getting to know Jimmy Carter
   - (B) Jimmy Carter was determined to someday enroll in the Navy and go to college.
   - (C) The days following Jimmy Carter's presidency
   - (D) The perils of picking cotton

2. **Which of these statements supports the main idea of the article?**
   - (F) Cotton bolls are very sharp.
   - (G) Carter enrolled in the U.S. Naval Academy, where he studied nuclear physics.
   - (H) Cotton plants need irrigation.
   - (J) Jimmy Carter always wanted to become president.

3. **Which would be another good title for this reading?**
   - (A) Jimmy's Vow
   - (B) Path to the Presidency
   - (C) Poverty in Georgia
   - (D) From Rags to Riches

READING: COMPREHENSION

● Lesson 8: Recalling Details

Directions: Read each item carefully. Then choose the correct answer that corresponds to that choice.

Example

While the fire was probably a case of arson, the investigator could not seem to find all of the evidence he needed to connect the main suspect to the scene of the fire. In the end it was the suspect himself who provided the missing link to the crime.

A. **How was this case of arson finally solved?**
- (A) Due to the diligence of the investigator
- (B) Due to the suspect's own mistakes
- (C) A stroke of genius
- (D) The time of day confirmed the fire.

 Clue Skim the passage and then answer the questions. Refer back to the passage to find the answers. You don't have to reread the passage for each question.

● Practice

Fire Mystery

Oily rags packed tightly into a box or a silo filled with damp grain suddenly bursting into flames appear to be mysterious, for they have no apparent causes. But there is one cause of fire that many people don't understand or even think about — spontaneous combustion.

All fires are caused by the heat that is given off when oxygen combines with some material. Fast oxidation gives off much heat and light very quickly and causes things to burn. Slow oxidation gives off no light and very little heat, not nearly enough to cause a fire. But when this little bit of heat is trapped it can not escape into the air. Instead it builds up. As more and more oxidation occurs, more heat is trapped. As the material gets hotter it oxidizes faster, and the faster oxidation produces even more heat. Finally things get so hot that a fire starts. Damp or oily materials and powdery substances are the most likely things to produce spontaneous combustion because a little moisture makes them oxidize more quickly.

1. **Which of these materials is most likely to produce spontaneous combustion?**
- (A) wood
- (B) oily rags
- (C) aluminum foil
- (D) hot rocks

2. **Which of these is not good advice for storing combustible materials?**
- (F) tightly packed box
- (G) loosely packed box
- (H) stored only when completely dry
- (J) stored in open containers

3. **Which is the best description of spontaneous combustion?**
- (A) oxygen combining with some material
- (B) no light and little heat given off
- (C) materials get so hot they explode into flames
- (D) much heat and some light

READING: COMPREHENSION

● Lesson 9: Inferences

Directions: Read each item. Choose the best answer and fill in the circle that corresponds to that choice.

Example

Ray stayed after school to finish some research he needed from the library. He missed the bus and now he needs to find a way home. He tries to call his older brother on his cell phone, but Randy's phone is not turned on. After quickly considering his options, Ray decides his best option is the following:

A.
- (A) Call his father at work and ask him to pick him up at school on the way home.
- (B) Even though the walk is over seven miles, he probably should start walking.
- (C) He should go through the building looking for a teacher who might be headed his way.
- (D) He should plan on spending the night at school.

 Skim the passage. Then read the questions. Refer back to the passage to find the answers. You don't have to reread the passage for each question.

● Practice

A Letter Home

Dear Mom,

I would have written sooner, but we have been busy. If you have been able to go to the movies, you probably saw it all on the Movietone newsreels.

How was Thanksgiving? Did Uncle Aubrey have enough gas rations to come? Our cooks did a good job here. All day long, I was sniffing all those good smells coming from the galley. We had sausage dressing, though, and not your special cornbread dressing. How is my sister? I can't believe that a year ago the two of us were leaving the house together and walking the railroad tracks to high school. Tell her, if she sees Betty at school to tell her Ray was thinking about her.

1. **Which of these ages do you think comes closest to Ray's age when he wrote the letter?**
   - (A) 15
   - (B) 17
   - (C) 19
   - (D) 29

2. **During which of these time periods do you think it is most probable that this letter was composed?**
   - (F) The Great Depression
   - (G) World War II
   - (H) Vietnam War
   - (J) Desert Storm

READING: COMPREHENSION

● Lesson 10: Fact and Opinion

Directions: Read each item carefully. Then choose the correct answer and fill in the circle that corresponds to that choice.

Examples

The Constitutional Convention met with the idea of revising the Articles of Confederation. There were many disagreements between the large and small states concerning the balance of power. In the end it was decided to create an entirely new document that would satisfy both sides.

A. **Which of the following is not a fact?**

  Ⓐ There were disagreements between the small and large states.

  Ⓑ A Constitutional Committee did meet.

  Ⓒ The Articles of Confederation had no value whatsoever.

  Ⓓ The Articles of Confederation had been the framework of the government.

Clue Skim the passage and then answer the questions. Refer back to the passage to find the answers. You don't have to reread the passage for each question.

● Practice

Young Inventors

If you are learning to play the guitar, you might have reason to thank Nicholas Ravagni. Ravagni owns a patent that helps new guitar players figure out where to place their fingers. Ravagni obtained his patent when he was 11. He got the idea for his invention when he was only six. He designed a self-adhesive and color-coded strip of plastic that fits under a guitar's strings.

You can thank other young inventors for everyday products. Open your refrigerator. You can probably find leftovers wrapped in aluminum foil. Thank Charles Hall, a college student who began experimenting with a process to create a cheap and ready supply of aluminum. When you tune in to your favorite FM radio station, thank Edwin Armstrong. Just after the turn of the century, Armstrong read a book about inventions.

Only 15, he decided that he would become an inventor of radios. By the time he was in his early twenties, he had made discoveries that would lead to his development of the FM radio.

1. **Which of the following is a fact?**

  Ⓐ Edwin Armstrong's inventions were more important than those of Charles Hall.

  Ⓑ Hall and Armstrong would advise children to have faith in their own abilities.

  Ⓒ Hall should have gotten better grades when he was in college.

  Ⓓ Ravagni was the youngest of these inventors to obtain his first patent.

READING: COMPREHENSION

● Lesson 11: Nonfiction

Directions: Read each item carefully. Then choose the correct answer and fill in the circle that corresponds to that choice.

Examples

Many of our great presidents are recognized for their deeds by placing their faces on U.S. coins. While President Lincoln is depicted on a penny, Thomas Jefferson's face is on a nickel. President Roosevelt's face is on a dime and the face of George Washington is found on quarters.

A.   This passage is about
- Ⓐ The value of having presidents on coins
- Ⓑ The importance of George Washington
- Ⓒ The presidents whose faces appear on coins
- Ⓓ The value of collecting coins

● **Practice** Here is a story about a man who loved adventure. Read the story and then answer questions 1 through 7.

Conquering Everest

Edmund Hillary first discovered mountain climbing on a school field trip. He loved climbing right away and would climb the local mountains at every opportunity. To climb safely, a person must be strong and reliable; Edmund was both. By the time he was in his twenties, Edmund was recognized for his mountaineering talents and had mastered many difficult feats. The young climber then decided to try some mountains in Europe. Through his adventures there, Edmund met Sir John Hunt, who was planning an expedition to Mount Everest. Situated on the border of Nepal and Tibet, the 29,028-foot-high peak had never been climbed successfully. Hunt quickly invited Edmund to go along on the trip, and the result was history. On May 29, 1953, Edmund and his Nepalese guide, Tenzing Norgay, were the first

people to reach the summit of the world's tallest mountain.

Edmund was responsible for setting up supply areas around the South Pole. To do this, he drove farm tractors to the supply sites and left the food and fuel behind. When he had finished the deliveries he drove all the way to the South Pole. Edmund's skilled management of the assignment helped the team attain its goal.

For the next twenty years Edmund continued to climb in the Himalayas. During this time, he came to know and depend on the Sherpas, the Nepalese people. Edmund's concern and appreciation for the Sherpas was so great that he raised money to build schools and hospitals for them, even helping with the construction.

GO ON ⇨

READING COMPREHENSION

● Lesson 11: Nonfiction (cont.)

Because of his many accomplishments and his dedication to human and environmental rights, Edmund received honorary degrees and decorations. He was also knighted in 1953. Sir Edmund Hillary accomplished much in his life. He is important not only because of his outdoor achievements, but because of his dedication to the things he believed in.

1. This excerpt is mostly about a person who—

(A) had dreams of becoming famous.

(B) fought his way out of poverty.

(C) was able to succeed despite many handicaps.

(D) achieved greatness in several arenas.

2. Who accompanied Sir Edmund Hillary on his most famous climb?

(F) Sir Vivian Fuchs

(G) a Hindu guide

(H) a Nepalese guide

(J) no one—he did it alone

3. According to what you read, which of these statements would Sir Edmund Hillary probably support?

(A) We should explore nature responsibly.

(B) People have the right to use nature as they wish.

(C) It is more important to take than to give.

(D) If you think you can't do something, don't try to do it.

4. Which is an opinion?

(F) Hillary was the greatest mountain climber ever.

(G) Hillary scaled Mt. Everest.

(H) Hillary was knighted.

(J) Mt. Everest is on the border of Nepal and Tibet.

5. While Hillary enjoyed adventures all over the earth, the scene of his greatest achievement was probably—

(A) Mt. Everest.

(B) the Amazon River.

(C) Mt. Lemmon.

(D) the Andes Mountains.

6. The word _decorations_, as it is used in the paragraph, probably means—

(F) ways to make a place look nice.

(G) awards or honors.

(H) ribbons and bows.

(J) lights and ornaments.

7. Choose the answer that best explains why Hillary built schools and hospitals for the Sherpas.

(A) It was part of his job as high commissioner.

(B) He wanted to prove that he could build things.

(C) He wanted to do something for them.

(D) He did it so they would keep helping him.

Name _____   Date_____

● **Lesson 12: Nonfiction**

Directions: Read each item carefully. Then choose the correct answer and fill in the circle that corresponds to that choice.

Example

The waffle cone was an invention of chance. During a fair in St. Louis, an ice cream vendor ran out of the paper bowls he was using to serve the ice cream. In the booth next to his was a vendor selling sweet pastries cooked on a waffle iron. The ice cream man bought some of the waffles and began serving ice cream in them. The waffle cone was born.

A.   This passage was all about—
- Ⓐ the invention of ice cream.
- Ⓑ the birth of the waffle cone.
- Ⓒ a cold treat at the fair.
- Ⓓ the first ice cream sundae.

Clue Skim the passage. Then answer the questions. Refer back to the passage to find the answers. You don't have to reread the story for each question.

● **Practice**

Tent Canvas Turned Overalls

In the mid-1800s, two chance events occurred in the life of a young "gold rusher" that resulted in the creation of the world's first pair of jeans. Twenty-three-year-old Levi Strauss, a Bavarian immigrant working at his brothers' dry goods store in New York City, did not join the gold rush because he wanted to stake a claim. He wanted to sell supplies to the men and women who did.

So in January of 1853, Levi Strauss acquired a waterfront building in San Francisco and began selling dry goods and Strauss Brothers products as his brothers' West Coast distributor. Business went well for him. Strauss ran an honest operation and became a wealthy and well-respected man.

Then the first chance occurrence that led to the availability of jeans presented itself to

Levi. Mr. Strauss imagined that the gold miners he catered to would require denim canvas with which to build tents and cover Conestoga wagons. He was wrong. Pleasant California weather persuaded miners to sleep directly under the stars. Levi would have to find another use for his yards and yards of brown denim canvas. The first generation of jeans was born. They were christened "waist overalls."

Then the second chance event occurred. Jacob Davis, a Nevada tailor who frequently bought bolts of cloth at Levi Strauss & Co., invented a method of strengthening the trousers. He placed metal rivets at pocket corners and at the base of the fly. He did not have the money to apply for a patent for his idea, so he sent Levi a letter. Perhaps Mr. Strauss would be interested in

GO ON

READING: COMPREHENSION

● Lesson 12: Nonfiction (cont.)

paying for the paperwork so that the two men could apply for the patent together. Strauss agreed. Rivets were added to the stress points of Levi's denim waist overalls, and the second generation of jeans was born. The term *jeans* was born out of the name of an Italian city, Genoa, where denim could be purchased.

Jeans did not change the life of Mr. Strauss significantly. He and Jacob Davis did earn good money from their successful riveted denim trousers, but Mr. Strauss was already a wealthy man. Denim jeans did significantly alter the lives for the rest of us. The Levi Strauss Company boasts that jeans are the only garment invented in the nineteenth century that are still worn today.

1. **The main idea of this reading is—**
   - (A) the California Gold Rush.
   - (B) the creation of the world's first pair of jeans.
   - (C) panning for gold in California.
   - (D) holding court in the Early West.

2. **The first chance occurrence in the creation of jeans was—**
   - (F) the lack of clothing by the miners.
   - (G) the interest of Jacob Davis in using rivets to strengthen the jeans.
   - (H) the mild weather in California which ruled out the market for denim.
   - (J) the building Strauss bought in San Francisco.

3. **Which offers the best conclusion to this success story?**
   - (A) Levi Strauss was fortunate to have been where he was when he was.
   - (B) Strauss was wealthy prior to creating his denim jeans.
   - (C) Conestoga wagons helped bring miners to California.
   - (D) Jacob Davis was very jealous of the success of Strauss.

4. **Which is not a fact?**
   - (F) Strauss was a Bavarian immigrant.
   - (G) The first jeans of Strauss were called "waist overalls."
   - (H) Both Levi Strauss and Jacob Davis applied for the patent.
   - (J) Strauss was fortunate to have a friend like Jacob Davis.

5. **The setting for this passage is—**
   - (A) Bavaria.
   - (B) Southern California.
   - (C) San Francisco area.
   - (D) New York City.

6. **The time setting for this passage could best be described as—**
   - (F) the early 1900s.
   - (G) the 1850s.
   - (H) the 1700s.
   - (J) the 1820s.

READING: COMPREHENSION

● Lesson 13: Nonfiction

Directions: Read each item carefully. Then choose the correct answer and fill in the circle that corresponds to that choice.

Example

Freezing retards the growth of molds, yeasts, bacteria, and enzymes in foods. However it is not the only method of preserving <u>perishables</u>. Dehydrating, canning, pickling, and applying chemical additives are additional methods of preserving the freshness, appearance, and nutritional value of foods.

A. **Which of the following best defines the underlined word in the passage to the left?**

- Ⓐ foods likely to spoil
- Ⓑ freeze-dried foods
- Ⓒ frozen foods
- Ⓓ pickled foods

● **Practice** **Clue** Skim the passage and then answer the questions. Refer back to the passage to find the answers. You don't have to reread the passage for each question.

Matthew Brady's Plan to End Warfare

Matthew Brady opened his first photography studio in 1844. The images produced were daguerreotypes, recorded images on sheets of copper coated with silver. They required long exposures to produce the image. A person being photographed would have to stay perfectly still for three to fifteen minutes. That made daguerreotypes impractical for portraits. By 1855, though, Brady was advertising a new type of image that had just been invented: a photograph made on paper.

From the beginning of his career, Brady thought that photography could serve an important purpose. His images could create a record of national life. When the Civil War broke out, he wanted to document the war. Although his costs were prohibitive and his friends discouraged him, he assembled a corps of photographers. He also bought photographs from others returning from the field. His efforts culminated in an 1862 display of photographs made after the Battle of Antietam. The bloodshed shocked the exhibit's visitors, most of whom had never known what warfare was like.

His goal was to use powerful photos to end all war. Brady did not stop warfare, of course. He did not even earn enough money to pay for his venture. After the Civil War, people lost interest in his chronicle of the war. He found few buyers for the photographs. He went bankrupt. Years after the war, Congress bought his collection, but he earned only enough money to pay the debts that had built up while he assembled the collection.

Still, Brady recorded one of the most important episodes in American history. In doing so, he created the first photo-documentation of a war.

GO ON

Name _____   Date _____

READING: COMPREHENSION

● Lesson 13: Nonfiction (cont.)

1. **The main idea of this passage is—**
   - (A) Matthew Brady's photographs.
   - (B) the Civil War.
   - (C) the plan of Matthew Brady to end warfare.
   - (D) portrait photography in the 1800s.

2. **The new technology that helped Brady to photograph real life was—**
   - (F) the daguerreotype.
   - (G) photographs made on paper.
   - (H) digital images.
   - (J) photosynthesis.

3. **Which of these occupations would best describe Matthew Brady's work?**
   - (A) combat soldier
   - (B) portrait photographer
   - (C) photojournalist
   - (D) wedding photographer

4. **Matthew Brady went bankrupt because—**
   - (F) his photographs weren't very good.
   - (G) there were few buyers for his photographs.
   - (H) other photographers had already done the same thing.
   - (J) he was never paid by Congress.

5. **The time setting for this passage on Matthew Brady was—**
   - (A) the 1500s.
   - (B) the 1600s.
   - (C) the 1700s.
   - (D) the 1800s.

6. **Brady wanted his photos to—**
   - (F) create a record of national life.
   - (G) create a pathway for young photographers.
   - (H) develop a school for Hudson River photography.
   - (J) set a standard for excellence in portrait photography.

7. **Daguerreotypes are images recorded on—**
   - (A) typing paper.
   - (B) copper sheets.
   - (C) silver nitrate.
   - (D) plaster.

STOP

━━━━━ *READING: COMPREHENSION* ━━━━━

● **Lesson 14: Reading Informational Text**

Directions: Read the letter. Choose the best answer for each question that follows.

Writing the Declaration of Independence

Letter From John Adams to Timothy Pickering, 1822

. . . Mr. Jefferson came into Congress in June, 1775, and brought with him a reputation for literature, science, and a happy talent of composition. Writings of his were handed about, remarkable for the peculiar felicity of expression. Though a silent member in Congress, he was so prompt, frank, explicit, and decisive upon committees and in conversation—not even Samuel Adams was more so—that he soon seized upon my heart; and upon this occasion I gave him my vote, and did all in my power to procure the votes of others. I think he had one more vote than any other, and that placed him at the head of the committee. I had the next highest number, and that placed me the second. The committee met, discussed the subject, and then appointed Mr. Jefferson and me to make the draft, I suppose because we were the two first on the list.

The subcommittee met. Jefferson proposed to me to make the draft. I said, "I will not, you should do it."

"Oh! No."

"Why will you not? You ought to do it."

"I will not."

"Why?"

"Reasons enough."

"What can be your reasons?"

"Reason first, you are a Virginian, and a Virginian ought to appear at the head of this business. Reason second, I am obnoxious, suspected, and unpopular. You are very much otherwise. Reason third, you can write ten times better than I can."

"Well," said Jefferson, "if you are decided, I will do as well as I can."

"Very well. When you have drawn it up, we will have a meeting."

A meeting we accordingly had, and conned the paper over. I was delighted with its high tone and the flights of oratory with which it abounded, especially that concerning Negro slavery, which, though I knew his Southern brethren would never suffer to pass in Congress, I certainly never would oppose. There were other expressions which I would not have inserted if I had drawn it up, particularly that which called the King tyrant. I thought this too personal, for I never believed George to be a tyrant in disposition and in nature; I always believed him to be deceived by his courtiers on both sides of the Atlantic, and in his official capacity, only, cruel. I thought the expression too passionate, and too much like scolding, for so grave and solemn a document; but as Franklin and Sherman were to inspect it afterwards, I thought it would not become me to strike it out. I consented to report it, and do not now remember that I made or suggested a single alteration. . . .

GO ON ⟶

READING: COMPREHENSION

● **Lesson 14: Reading Informational Text (cont.)**

1. **How does the letter illustrate that Jefferson and Samuel Adams had similar personalities?**

   (A) Jefferson's decisive nature is compared with Samuel Adams's.

   (B) Jefferson and Samuel Adams both disliked Timothy Pickering.

   (C) Samuel Adams coached Jefferson as he drafted the document.

   (D) Both Jefferson and Samuel Adams represented Virginia.

2. **A portion of the letter's first paragraph reads *Though a silent member in Congress, he was so prompt, frank, explicit, and decisive. . .that he soon seized upon my heart.***

   How does this statement show how Jefferson influenced John Adams?

   (F) It shows that Jefferson caused Adams physical discomfort.

   (G) It emphasizes the respect Adams had for Jefferson.

   (H) It conveys Jefferson's talents and capabilities.

   (J) It exaggerates Jefferson's talents and capabilities.

3. **Based on the letter, John Adams's point of view about his own contributions to the *Declaration of Independence* could be described as**

   (A) confused.

   (B) relieved.

   (C) anxious.

   (D) modest.

4. **The letter's central idea is expressed by which statement?**

   (F) Pickering edited the *Declaration of Independence*.

   (G) John Adams admired and respected Jefferson.

   (H) Jefferson disagreed with Pickering.

   (J) Both Jefferson and Pickering disliked King George.

5. **What does John Adams convey when he writes the following?**

   Reason second, I am obnoxious, suspected, and unpopular. You are very much otherwise.

   (A) discomfort over collaborating with Jefferson on the first draft

   (B) embarrassment about his reputation

   (C) suspicion that Pickering was not asked to write the first draft

   (D) opposition with Jefferson

GO ON

READING: COMPREHENSION

● Lesson 14: Reading Informational Text (cont.)

6. **John Adams persuades Jefferson to write the *Declaration of Independence* and provides several reasons for his argument. Which piece of evidence from the text is irrelevant to Jefferson's qualifications to draft the document?**

    (F) Jefferson had a happy talent of composition.

    (G) Jefferson received enough votes to place him at the head of the writing subcommittee.

    (H) As a member in Congress, Jefferson was often silent.

    (J) Jefferson was a Virginian.

7. **John Adams describes himself as *obnoxious, suspected, and unpopular*. How does this description affect the impact of Adams's letter to Pickering?**

    (A) It gives the letter a sarcastic tone, and reveals Adams's jealousy of Jefferson.

    (B) It exaggerates Adams's self-confidence.

    (C) It reveals that Adams did not feel qualified to participate in government.

    (D) It lightens the tone of the letter while revealing Adams's regard for Jefferson's abilities.

8. **How does John Adams acknowledge that his view of slavery is different from that of many Southern members?**

    (F) Adams appreciates that Jefferson's draft mentions concerns about slavery.

    (G) Adams writes about his disagreements with Southern committee members.

    (H) Adams disagrees with Jefferson's point of view regarding slavery.

    (J) Adams alters the changes that Southern committee members make regarding slavery.

9. **Based on the letter, which word best describes John Adams?**

    (A) suspicious

    (B) indecisive

    (C) happy

    (D) humble

10. **Choose the sentence that provides sufficient evidence to support Adams's belief that King George was not a tyrant.**

    (F) John Adams was a member of the Continental Congress, and he opposed King George.

    (G) King George opposed members of the Continental Congress.

    (H) Close advisors deceived King George.

    (J) Thomas Jefferson regarded King George unfavorably.

STOP

READING: COMPREHENSION

● Lesson 15: Story Elements

Directions: Read each item carefully. Then choose the correct answer and fill in the circle that corresponds to that choice.

Example

When the two boys reached the mouth of the cave, Tommy told Mike that he would need a flashlight. "Rats!" Mike exclaimed. "I left mine in my backpack."

A.   The setting for this story is
- (A) Tommy and Mike
- (B) The mouth of the cave
- (C) The forgotten flashlight
- (D) Mike's backpack

● Practice   Skim the passage. Then answer the questions. Refer back to the passage to find the answers. You don't have to reread the passage for each question.

I Wasn't So Sure!

Mom said the smell of a summer morning from the ground up was worth all the ants that shared your food, but I wasn't so sure. She said that the wilderness would teach a boy how to make decisions like a man. I thought she was being silly. Funny how you get surprised.

It was my fault. One of those manly choices, when all I wanted to be was a little boy. All I could think about was swimming. I didn't want to pick the tent spot. So when I found one with just a few mounds of dirt I stomped down the mounds and was swimming in no time. It wasn't until later that we met our tent mates. I climbed into my sleeping bag. I ignored the first few bites, kicking whatever was at the bottom of my bag. Shortly, Mom crawled into her bag. I heard her kick the bottom of her sleeping bag too. Soon I heard her roll over and slap her arm.

"What is in these bags?" she demanded. "I'm getting eaten alive." I switched on the flashlight, aiming it at her bag. Swarming in the light's circular glow were hundreds of tiny red ants.

Mom said, "I think you found an ant hill!" She grabbed her keys and headed for the car. Now, I'm more careful when I pick a tent site.

1.   The setting for this story is a—
- (A) river.
- (B) scout camp.
- (C) lake.
- (D) beach.

2.   What is the main reason for his mother coming along on the camping trip?
- (F) to tuck him in at night
- (G) to help him learn how to become a man by making decisions in the wilderness
- (H) to drive him
- (J) to cook his food

3.   Which offers the best lesson learned by the main character?
- (A) to make good decisions
- (B) to stay in a motel
- (C) to bring along ant spray
- (D) to trust his mother

STOP

READING: COMPREHENSION

● **Lesson 16: Fiction**

Directions: Read each item carefully. Then choose the correct answer and fill in the circle that corresponds to that choice.

Example

The museum was a treat for my senses. The paintings had colors that tickled my eyes. I enjoyed listening to the guide's happy voice when she talked about the artists. And even though we weren't allowed to touch anything, I could feel the pictures in my mind. The guide told us that some artists mainly like to paint nature while others prefer painting people or interesting designs.

A. **The author in this story is telling us about—**

(A) museums.
(B) fire safety at the museum.
(C) the enjoyment experienced during a visit to an art museum.
(D) the colors that appeal to the senses.

 Skim the passage and then answer the questions. Refer back to the passage to find the answers. You don't have to reread the passage for each question.

● **Practice**

They Had It So Good!

"Eighth grade is just killing me!" complained Bo. "There's one test after another, teachers yelling, pressure from parents to get good grades. You'd think we were seniors in high school. I mean, we have four more years after this one! Maybe I don't even want to go to college.

"We're living in the wrong time. I wish we lived in the 1800s. Kids didn't go to school much, especially those who lived on farms."

Emily came over. "I couldn't help hearing," she said. "And, far be it for me to burst your little bubble, but I wouldn't want to be a pioneer." Everybody sort of rolled their eyes. Miss Know-it-all was about to impart her wisdom again.

Emily continued. "Pioneer families left their homes to travel in Conestoga wagons that would leak or break down. They would be attacked by Native Americans who didn't want more settlers taking their land. Horses would die, guides would desert them, there were bandits on the road, and chances were that even if they got where they were going, the land would be a big disappointment.

"The land might be rocky and not even worth farming. If the pioneers saw that the Native Americans were going to stay, they often just burned them out. Nobody ever asked the Native Americans permission to use their land, much less own it! Kids worked from sunup to sundown on these farms. Food might be scarce, so often all they'd get at dinner

GO ON

READING: COMPREHENSION

● Lesson 16: Fiction (cont.)

would be some watery stew or potatoes. Water was usually far from the house, so most people only bathed once a week if they were lucky.

"Doesn't sound so good, huh? Some places had no trees, so forget the cozy log house. A room dug into a hillside with sod for a roof might be the best you could do. And, you'd be so lonely for other people, you'd welcome school. Of course every grade would be taught in a one-room schoolhouse. There'd be no paper, just little blackboards. You might have to walk miles in the snow, and…"

Bo stood up and began to leave! "Enough!" he said. "Any more of this, and you'll have me being happy about school." Emily smiled. Another mission accomplished, she thought.

1. **The main idea of this passage is—**
   - (A) Bo's distaste for school.
   - (B) difficult times in pioneer days.
   - (C) kids only went to school when chores were done.
   - (D) Bo wanted to run away from home.

2. **All were disadvantages of going to school in pioneer days except—**
   - (F) the possibility of Indian attacks.
   - (G) travel to and from school was dangerous.
   - (H) the land was poor as were most of the people.
   - (J) there would not have been the pressure associated with today's expectations in school.

3. **After listening to Emily, Bo probably came to this conclusion.**
   - (A) Going to school today is a much better experience than it was in the 1800s.
   - (B) Pioneer children had it made.
   - (C) People didn't care much about their health in the 1800s.
   - (D) Kids today work much harder than children of the 1800s.

4. **Which is not a fact?**
   - (F) Emily's views on going to school were much better than Bo's.
   - (G) Children during the 1800s didn't go to school for as long as children today.
   - (H) Pioneers faced many dangers during the 1800s.
   - (J) There is more pressure on children to succeed in today's schools.

5. **The main characters are—**
   - (A) the pioneers and the Indians.
   - (B) school children during the 1800s.
   - (C) Bo and Emily.
   - (D) parents and teachers.

6. **What grade are these students in?**
   - (F) seventh
   - (G) eighth
   - (H) ninth

7. **The early pioneers traveled west in—**
   - (A) Conestoga wagons.
   - (B) family cars.
   - (C) horse-drawn carriages.
   - (D) mule-drawn carts.

READING: COMPREHENSION

● Lesson 17: Fiction

Directions: Read each item carefully. Then choose the correct answer and fill in the circle that corresponds to that choice.

Example

Courtney needed a summer job, so she responded to an ad in the local newspaper for someone to stock shelves. Courtney was pleased when she was called in for an interview. On her way to the interview, she wondered what she would be stocking on those shelves. She was delighted to find out that it was a music store as CDs were among her favorite things.

A.   What is a fact from the passage?

Ⓐ Courtney liked country music as much as anyone.

Ⓑ Courtney was granted an interview for the job.

Ⓒ Stocking CDs is much better work than stocking DVDs.

Ⓓ Anyone can get a job from a newspaper ad.

Clue Skim the passage. Then answer the questions. Refer back to the passage to find the answers. You don't have to reread the passage for each question.

● Practice

One Step at a Time

Tracy studied the girls ahead of her, numbers pinned to each hunter-green shirt. Tracy's was kelly green. She bit her lip. "Don't worry about everything all at once," her grandmother always told her. "Break each problem into little steps."

How? No way was she going to be able to smile. Her back tucks had been so low yesterday that she'd landed on her knees. She'd been chanting too fast all week. One step at a time, she told herself, but her chest tightened.

The gym door opened, and a girl slipped inside. Tracy heard a faint "Go, Eagles!" What if she started before the judges gave her the signal? She shook her head. Worry about the tumbling. Impossible to break even that into separate steps. She had to get her timing

right, keep her feet together, remember not to make duck hands. She moaned, stepping out of line.

"Where are you going?" the girl behind her said. "You're next."

Next? The gym door opened. The girl pushed Tracy inside. The judges sat at a table all the way across the polished gym floor. Tracy swallowed. She was going to throw up. She was going to faint. All those faces watching. All that distance to go.

She let her breath out in a long hiss, then took off. Halfway into her hurdle, she remembered that she hadn't yelled, hadn't made any hand signals. She pitched forward, then caught herself. Her heart thundered, and she couldn't move. Just go forward, she

GO ON →

32

READING: COMPREHENSION

● Lesson 17: Fiction (cont.)

told herself. Just take the first step. On the second flip-flop, she realized she was rebounding high enough. She hurled herself through the back tuck, landing on both feet. She grinned, yelled "Go, Eagles," then ran forward. One step at a time.

1.   What is the main idea in the passage?

- (A) Tracy's self esteem
- (B) Tracy trying to remember her routine
- (C) The advice of Tracy's grandmother for solving problems
- (D) Tracy becomes a cheerleader for the Eagles

2.   Tracy's first worry was—

- (F) to land on her feet.
- (G) to cheer for the Eagles.
- (H) to make a graceful flip in the middle of the routine.
- (J) the tumbling.

3.   Once Tracy completes her tumbling routine and shouts, "Go, Eagles," we think—

- (A) she is going to become a cheerleader.
- (B) she still lacks in self-esteem.
- (C) she needs to try harder.
- (D) she needs to get another hobby.

4.   Which is an opinion?

- (F) The judges sat across the gym floor.
- (G) Tracy was very nervous about her tryout.
- (H) Tracy had a number pinned to her green shirt.
- (J) Her grandmother had some very sound advice for solving problems.

5.   The main character in this passage is—

- (A) Tracy's grandmother.
- (B) Tracy's sister.
- (C) Tracy.
- (D) the judges.

6.   What color was Tracy's shirt?

- (F) red
- (G) blue
- (H) gold
- (J) green

7.   What was the school's nickname?

- (A) Wildcats
- (B) Hoosiers
- (C) Rams
- (D) Eagles

READING: COMPREHENSION

● **Lesson 18: Fiction**

Directions: Read each item carefully. Then choose the correct answer and fill in the circle that corresponds to that choice.

Example

I have just finished my trip down the Congo River and am applying for entrance to your club. I have the $1,000 entry fee and am including the tale and photographs of an amazing adventure. This tale demonstrates my ability to face challenges. I hope you accept me.

A. **What is the goal of the person who wrote this letter?**

(A) to travel the entire length of the Congo River

(B) to become a member of the Congo Club

(C) to win the $1,000 prize for best entry

(D) to see the Congo River from a helicopter

 Skim the passage and then answer the questions. Refer back to the passage to find the answers. You don't have to reread the passage for each question.

● **Practice**

Letter to the Governor

Dear Governor,

I am a 12-year-old Native American who is in the seventh grade. I grew up on a reservation, but this year my family moved to Tucson because my mom thinks the schools here are better for me. I miss my home a lot. One thing I really miss is being able to drive.

I am writing to you because I think the minimum age for getting a driver's license in our state is way too high. Why do we have to be 16 before we can get a license? We can't even get a driver's permit until we are 15 1/2. It is unfair because kids are just as able to drive as adults. They just need the chance to learn.

I know this because I know how to drive. So do my friends on the reservation. We practiced in the fields and on the back roads, and now we are all good drivers. If I had a driver's license, I could get around more easily because I would not need to beg others for rides. Please consider lowering the minimum age for getting a driver's license.

Sincerely yours,

Maria Miguel

GO ON

READING: COMPREHENSION

● **Lesson 18: Fiction (cont.)**

1. **Which is the main idea of this letter to the governor?**
   - (A) to drive a car the entire length of the state of Arizona
   - (B) to obtain a driver's license to drive around the reservation
   - (C) to get a driver's license at the age of 12
   - (D) to lower the age for getting a driver's license to 15

2. **Which expresses the feelings of the writer?**
   - (F) She feels the age of getting a driver's license is unfair.
   - (G) She doesn't want to live on the reservation any more.
   - (H) She doesn't want to go to school in Tucson.
   - (J) She prefers driving a Jeep to a Honda.

3. **Why do you think the young Native American wants her license?**
   - (A) She wants to show other children how well she can drive a car.
   - (B) She thinks she can drive as well as adults because of her experience.
   - (C) She wants a new car.
   - (D) She prefers driving to school to wearing a pair of roller skates.

4. **Which is a fact?**
   - (F) Native Americans are the best drivers.
   - (G) The earlier you learn to drive, the better driver you become.
   - (H) Young children are better drivers than adults.
   - (J) This 12-year old was allowed to drive on the reservation.

5. **The main character in this passage is—**
   - (A) a Native American.
   - (B) a California drifter.
   - (C) a parent from Illinois.
   - (D) an auto mechanic.

6. **What city does this young girl now call home?**
   - (F) New York City
   - (G) Cleveland
   - (H) Los Angeles
   - (J) Tucson

7. **Where did she learn how to drive?**
   - (A) driver's education program at school
   - (B) from a private driver education program
   - (C) on a reservation
   - (D) in Tucson, Arizona

READING: COMPREHENSION

● **Lesson 19: Reading Literature**

Directions: Read the story. Choose the best answers to the questions that follow.

The Escape

Into the shady glen the small figure rode on a pony little larger than a dog. The pony's breath misted in the crisp air as the beast blew air out of its nostrils. The green-mantled figure patted the neck of the beast, whispering words of comfort into the animal's ear. In response, the faithful steed nickered, thumped his wide hoofs twice upon the soft bed of the forest floor, and ceased its shaking.

"We've left the raiders behind, old friend," said Rowan, as she removed her hooded mantle and tossed her head back and forth, bringing peace to her own troubled mind. Rowan was one of four daughters of Sylvia, guide of all wood folk.

Suddenly, shouts of rough men cut through the glade's peace.

"In here, I tell ya. The maid's gone to hiding in this grove."

"Nah, ya lunk. She'd never wait for us here. Not after she dunked old Stefan at the marsh. No! She's a gone on to her crazy folk, don'tcha know."

The two gray-cloaked riders dismounted, still arguing as they examined the earth for traces of the child's flight.

"Who was the lout who let her escape?" asked the first.

"'Tis one who no longer breathes the air so freely," returned the second grimly. "The lord nearly choked the fool, even as the knave begged for mercy. Ah, there's little patience for one who lets a mystic escape, to be true!"

Five nobly dressed horsemen wove through the trees to the clearing where these two rustics still squatted. In the lead came the fierce lord, a huge form with scarlet and gray finery worn over his coat of mail.

"What say you?" he roared. "Have you found the trail of Rowan?"

"No, sire," spoke the first gray, trembling, "though I was certain the child headed into this wood. Shall I continue to search, lord?"

"Aye, indeed," replied the master calmly, controlled. "She is here. I know it, too. You have a keen sense for the hunt, Mikkel. Be at ready with your blade. And you too, Short Brush! Though a child, our Rowan is vicious with her weapon."

"Yes, sire," agreed Mikkel and Short Brush.

The two grays beat the bushes in the search. Closer and closer they came to the child's hiding place, a small earthen scoop created when the roots of a wind-blown tree pulled free of the earth.

GO ON

READING: COMPREHENSION

● Lesson 19: Reading Literature (cont.)

The evil lord and his lot remained mounted, ready to pursue should the young girl determine to take flight once more. And so, they were not prepared for the child's play.

Rowan softly, softly sang, "You wind-whipped branches sudder, shake. You oaks and cedars, tremble. Take these men and beasts who do us wrong. Not in these woods do they belong.

As a mighty gust of wind roared, nearby trees slapped their branches to the point of breaking, reaching out and grasping the five mounted men. An immense gaping cavern opened in the trunk of an ancient oak and swallowed the five surprised mail-clad men whole.

Mikkel and Short Brush, too, were lifted high into the air by a white pine and a blue spruce. Lifted high. Kept high. For a while.

"Return from whence you came. Go to your families, and tell them of the wrath of Sylvia," commanded Rowan. "She would not wish you to come to her land again!"

The pine and spruce tossed the two gray trackers over the trees of the forest and into the field beyond. The field was already harvested and soggy with the rains of autumn. Mikkel and Short Brush, unhurt but shaken by their arboreal flight, rose and fled immediately to tell their master of the strange doings of this wood.

1. **This story belongs to the fantasy genre. Which classic story fits this genre?**
   - (A) *The Diary of a Young Girl* by Anne Frank
   - (B) *The Lord of the Rings* trilogy by J.R.R. Tolkien
   - (C) *A Wrinkle in Time* by Madeleine L'Engle
   - (D) Sherlock Holmes stories by Sir Arthur Conan Doyle

2. **In writing the sentence *And so, they were not prepared for the child's play*, why might the author have used *play* instead of another verb to describe Rowan's actions?**
   - (F) *Play* connotes a particularly clever move.
   - (G) *Play* is used to suggest humor.
   - (H) *Play* is an exaggeration of the action that follows.
   - (J) *Play* connotes a particularly cowardly act.

3. **Mikkel and Short Brush flee the woods after the trees toss them onto the field. Readers would probably describe this as humorous. Mikkel and Short Brush would probably describe this as**
   - (A) frightening.
   - (B) ordinary.
   - (C) happy.
   - (D) peaceful.

GO ON

READING: COMPREHENSION

● **Lesson 19: Reading Literature (cont.)**

4. **The raiders pursue Rowan because she**
   - (F) has lost her way in the woods.
   - (G) has stolen their steed.
   - (H) has discovered the raiders' hiding place.
   - (J) has escaped from them.

5. **Which best describes the story's theme?**
   - (A) rich versus poor
   - (B) good versus evil
   - (C) beauty versus ugliness
   - (D) old versus new

6. *Closer and closer they came to the child's hiding place, a small earthen scoop created when the roots of a wind-blown tree pulled free of the earth.*

   Which best describes how Rowan and the reader feel at this point in the passage's action?
   - (F) Rowan finds it humorous, while the reader finds it happy.
   - (G) Rowan finds it suspenseful, while the reader finds it peaceful.
   - (H) Rowan finds it satisfying, while the reader finds it suspenseful.
   - (J) Rowan finds it ordinary, while the reader finds it humorous.

7. **By describing the lord as adorned in *finery*, the author**
   - (A) emphasizes the lord's high ranking.
   - (B) ridicules the dress of the lord's subjects.
   - (C) reveals that the lord dressed for just this occasion.
   - (D) contrasts the lord's wealth with Rowan's low ranking.

8. **Why does Rowan cast a spell?**
   - (F) Rowan is determined to rescue Mikkel and Short Brush.
   - (G) The evil lord and his lot have almost discovered her.
   - (H) Mikkel and Short Brush captured Rowan's weapon.
   - (J) Rowan's pony is hungry and she needs to feed it.

9. **Which characters could best be described as *virtuous*?**
   - (A) the five nobly dressed horsemen
   - (B) Sylvia and the lord
   - (C) Mikkel and Short Brush
   - (D) Rowan and the other daughters of Sylvia

10. **What do Rowan's songs and the trees' reaction tell about her character?**
    - (F) Rowan is old and wise.
    - (G) Mikkel and Short Brush are her enemies.
    - (H) She is controlling otherworldly forces.
    - (J) She is working with the evil lord.

STOP

Name _____ Date_____

Directions: Read each item carefully. Then choose the correct answer and fill in the circle that corresponds to that choice.

Example

She had never been inside a mine shaft. She had no friends or relatives who worked as coal miners. The old dressmaker, who frequently wore a shawl and a bonnet, seemed a highly unlikely candidate for the position of motivator for the mine workers.

A. **Which of the following is a fact?**

  (A) Women make better miners than men.

  (B) Coal mining is a very dangerous business.

  (C) Women should not be allowed to wear a bonnet into the mine.

  (D) The woman in this passage had never been in a mine shaft.

Skim the passage and then answer the questions. Refer back to the passage to find the answers. You don't have to reread the passage for each question.

E-mail Alert

    U.S. Representative David McDavid today introduced Bill 409 to the House of Representatives. McDavid reports that Internet e-mail and instant messaging services cost the U.S. Postal Service in lost postage fees. Bill 409 would permit the U.S. Postal Service to charge a five-cent surcharge on each e-mail sent. The U.S. Postal Service would bill the Internet service provider, which would in turn charge the sender of the e-mail. Representative McDavid reports that no final decision has been made on charging for instant messaging services. This surcharge may be added to the bill at a later time. Attorney Ronald Sneed of Omaha, Nebraska, has agreed to fight this bill, filing a class-action suit on behalf of a group of frequent Internet users. Sneed has asked that citizens forward this e-mail to everyone on their mailing list, in order to alert citizens of this new charge.

1. **According to this alert, David McDavid is—**

  (A) a U.S. Congressman.

  (B) a U.S. Senator.

  (C) an interested citizen.

  (D) the Director of Consumer Affairs.

2. **The main concern of this article is—**

  (F) the role of Congress.

  (G) undocumented claims.

  (H) possible charges imposed by the U.S. Postal Service for e-mail messages.

  (J) there is no concern expressed in this article.

GO ON

READING: COMPREHENSION
SAMPLE TEST (cont.)

The Underwater Jungle

Can you imagine a wilderness under the sea that is so humongous it has never been fully explored? The Great Barrier Reef is such a place, being the largest ridge of coral in the world. It is 1,250 miles long—that's about as far as the distance between Detroit, Michigan, and Houston, Texas. Its undersea coral gardens provide homes for more than 1,400 varieties of exotic fish. This huge maritime province stretches along the northeastern coast of Australia and ranges from 10 to more than 100 miles from the shore.

In 1770, English explorer Captain James Cook discovered the reef on his way to Antarctica. His ship was the first of many to be damaged on the treacherous, sharp coral lying just below the ocean's surface. In fact, the reef is a graveyard to more than 500 ships. Navigational charts are marked in some places with the warning "Unexamined but considered dangerous to navigation." The weather causes other hazards to ships. Sometimes whole islands disappear in great storms called cyclones which change reef maps overnight.

Danger also lies down in the reef. Huge awesome creatures lurk in its crevices. Sea snakes with venom in their fangs swim with 10-foot moray eels. Sea crocodiles, sea turtles, giant clams, and 600-pound groper fish with a mythic reputation for eating people also reside among the coral. And, if that's not enough, manta rays, weighing four tons and having a wing span of 20 feet, keep company with 35-foot, extremely dangerous, white sharks. One resident, the 70-foot whale shark, is friendly. His diet consists of anchovies, without the pizza!

The reef is made up mainly of little animals called coral polyps, which are one-half inch or less long. Their colonies resemble multicolored flowers and vegetables. The greatest enemy of the polyps is the crown of thorns starfish. Named for the venomous spines of their bodies, these starfish are enormous eaters, and their favorite fast-food restaurant is the Great Barrier Reef. One starfish can strip the polyps from seven square feet of coral a week, leaving a wasteland behind. They are sometimes 24 inches in width with up to 23 arms. When they are chopped up, they regenerate. If an arm is cut off, it grows back! It's no wonder you can see up to 5,000 starfish in one small area! This starfish invasion is quite recent, large numbers having started to appear in the 1960s. One theory to explain this population explosion is that man-made pollution has somehow given starfish a survival edge over conditions that previously held their numbers down. But if humans try to radically interfere and stop the starfish, the situation could be made even worse. Interfering with nature often yields awful results.

This sea garden has problems other than starfish. Oil rigs, mining, wrecked ships, and tourists also harm the reef. Commercial interests, wishing to develop and mine the area, often grab up pieces as fast as the starfish.

GO ON

READING: COMPREHENSION
SAMPLE TEST (cont.)

The Australian government is working hard to keep the reef structures intact. The Great Barrier Reef Marine Park Authority has sea and air rangers. They believe the ecological balance must be preserved. Maybe one day you will be able to visit the reef.

3. What is the topic of the reading selection "The Underwater Jungle"?

(A) sea creatures

(B) the Great Barrier Reef

(C) wrecked ships

(D) starfish

4. What is the main idea of the second paragraph?

(F) The sharp coral and the weather cause hazards for ships.

(G) Captain Cook discovered the Great Barrier Reef.

(H) The Reef is a graveyard to 500 wrecked ships.

(J) Sometimes cyclones cause whole islands to disappear.

5. In paragraph three, which statement(s) support(s) the paragraph's main idea, "Danger also lies down in the Reef"?

(A) Sea snakes and moray eels live in the crevices.

(B) Manta rays and white sharks are found in the reef.

(C) Sea crocodiles, sea turtles, giant clams, and groper fish are residents.

(D) All of these choices.

6. What is the main idea of paragraph four?

(F) If a starfish loses an arm, it grows another.

(G) The crown of thorns starfish are destroying the reef.

(H) The reef is made up of coral polyps.

(J) Man-made pollution has helped the starfish population to explode.

7. Which of these statements is not true?

(A) The Great Barrier Reef Marine Park Authority has sea and air rangers.

(B) Captain James Cook discovered the Great Barrier Reef on his way to the Arctic.

(C) The Great Barrier Reef is 1,250 miles long.

(D) Crown of thorns starfish are sometimes two feet wide.

8. Which is not a danger to the Great Barrier Reef?

(F) crown of thorns starfish

(G) tourists

(H) oil rigs

(J) ecologists

9. Which of these inhabitants of the Great Barrier Reef does not pose a danger to humans?

(A) whale shark

(B) white shark

(C) sea crocodiles

(D) manta rays

GO ON

Great Faces in High Places

If you were driving in the Black Hills of South Dakota about 25 miles southwest of Rapid City and saw four faces on a mountain looking at you, you would not be seeing things! You would be viewing Mt. Rushmore, a national memorial with the images of four American Presidents carved in the mountain's granite.

The 60-foot heads of Presidents George Washington, Thomas Jefferson, Theodore Roosevelt, and Abraham Lincoln were chiseled in the 6,000-foot-high mountain by American sculptor Gutzon Borglum. He began his task in August of 1927 primarily using dynamite and a jackhammer to alter the mountain side.

He completed his first figure, Washington, for a dedication on July 4, 1930. Borglum died in 1941, but his son Lincoln was able to continue the work. Their studio still exists showcasing the Borglums' scale models, bits, chisels, hammers, and other tools.

It took 14 years to carve the faces on Mt. Rushmore, although only six and one-half were spent in actual work by the father and son. The job was held up by bad weather and lack of funds. The total cost was just under one million dollars, of which the federal government paid approximately 84%. Private donations made up the rest of the amount.

Over 2,000,000 people visit Mt. Rushmore each year to see the memorial that was first suggested in 1923 by Jonah Robinson of the South Dakota State Historical Society. The idea was approved, and the mountain was established as a national memorial in 1925.

The mountain was named after a New York lawyer, Charles E. Rushmore, who visited the area in 1885. Traveling through the area, he asked a prospector the name of the mountain and since it had no name, the prospector looked at the lawyer and said with a grin, "Rushmore." The name stuck.

Each of the heads on the mountain represent an aspect of the United States. Borglum selected George Washington to represent the founding of the nation, since he was the first President. Thomas Jefferson, the country's third President, wrote the Declaration of Independence and represents the nation's political philosophy. Abraham Lincoln, the 16th President, represents preservation of the nation. He was elected in 1861 and served during the United States' Civil War. He refused to let the nation be divided and brought about the emancipation of the slaves in the South. Theodore Roosevelt represents the expansion and conservation of the nation. After becoming the 26th President, his administration set aside 194,000,000 additional acres of land for parks and saved mineral, oil, coal, and waterpower sites for future generations.

Mount Rushmore, a marvel of artistic and engineering skill, demonstrates a belief Gutzon Borglum held: "A monument's dimensions should be determined by the importance to civilization of the events commemorated." The gigantic sculpture is awe-inspiring.

GO ON

READING: COMPREHENSION
SAMPLE TEST (cont.)

10. **What is the main idea of the selection?**
    - (F) man's dominance over nature
    - (G) a boost to South Dakota tourism
    - (H) a memorial to four great American presidents
    - (J) private donations for the public good

11. **Which of these American presidents is not etched in stone on Mt. Rushmore?**
    - (A) John F. Kennedy
    - (B) Abraham Lincoln
    - (C) Theodore Roosevelt
    - (D) George Washington

12. **Who was the sculptor of this great monument?**
    - (F) Claude Monet
    - (G) Gutzon Borglum
    - (H) Jonah Robinson
    - (J) Robinson William Caruso

13. **Which description is incorrect?**
    - (A) George Washington represents the founding of the nation.
    - (B) Abraham Lincoln represents the preservation of the nation.
    - (C) Theodore Roosevelt represents the expansion of the nation.
    - (D) Thomas Jefferson represents the poetry of the nation.

14. **The location of this great monument is—**
    - (F) near Kansas City, Missouri.
    - (G) near Rapid City, South Dakota.
    - (H) near Billings, Montana.
    - (J) near Cheyenne, Wyoming.

15. **Who among the following was the second sculptor to work on the monument?**
    - (A) Chandler Westinghouse
    - (B) Evan Fitzsimmons
    - (C) Lincoln Borglum
    - (D) Charles E. Rushmore

16. **How long did it take to complete the memorial from start to finish?**
    - (F) a full year
    - (G) three years
    - (H) ten years
    - (J) fourteen years

STOP

READING PRACTICE TEST

● **Part 1: Vocabulary**

Directions: For Example A, find the word that means the same as the underlined word. For Example B, find the word that means the opposite of the underlined word.

Examples

A.	**gruesome costume**	B.	**forthright opinion**
	(A) beautiful		(F) stealthy
	(B) exquisite		(G) sincere
	(C) ghastly		(H) honest
	(D) sublime		(J) genuine

For numbers 1–8, read each item. Choose the answer that means the same or about the same as the underlined word.

1. **gorgeous actress**
   - (A) homely
   - (B) talented
   - (C) beautiful
   - (D) dedicated

2. **an immaculate bedroom**
   - (F) jumbled
   - (G) unkempt
   - (H) tidy
   - (J) cluttered

3. **contribute to the charity**
   - (A) donate
   - (B) scramble
   - (C) reimburse
   - (D) work

4. **demolish the house**
   - (F) build
   - (G) destroy
   - (H) construct
   - (J) remodel

5. **exit the state**
   - (A) commence
   - (B) stand
   - (C) enter
   - (D) leave

6. **desolate land**
   - (F) lonely
   - (G) cozy
   - (H) fertile
   - (J) difficult

7. **intelligent student**
   - (A) tardy
   - (B) smart
   - (C) punctual
   - (D) hungry

8. **unbiased jury**
   - (F) relaxed
   - (G) impartial
   - (H) lonely
   - (J) prejudiced

GO ON

Name _____ Date_____

For numbers 9–16, read each item. Choose the answer that is the opposite of the underlined word.

9. **punctual student**
   - Ⓐ foolish
   - Ⓑ average
   - Ⓒ intelligent
   - Ⓓ tardy

10. **impoverished college student**
    - Ⓕ wealthy
    - Ⓖ poor
    - Ⓗ grateful
    - Ⓙ clumsy

11. **loud moan**
    - Ⓐ laugh
    - Ⓑ wail
    - Ⓒ shout
    - Ⓓ movement

12. **dishonest response**
    - Ⓕ hostile
    - Ⓖ candid
    - Ⓗ raucous
    - Ⓙ edited

13. **talkative**
    - Ⓐ gabby
    - Ⓑ garrulous
    - Ⓒ chatty
    - Ⓓ mute

14. **merge the documents**
    - Ⓕ separate
    - Ⓖ bring together
    - Ⓗ cast aside
    - Ⓙ edit

15. **a famine**
    - Ⓐ drought
    - Ⓑ time of plenty
    - Ⓒ escape
    - Ⓓ dedication

16. **irrelevant**
    - Ⓕ unnecessary
    - Ⓖ unimportant
    - Ⓗ nonessential
    - Ⓙ important

READING PRACTICE TEST
Part 1: Vocabulary (cont.)

For numbers 17–20, choose the word that best completes each sentence.

17. Mei and I _____ to spend the summer backpacking across Europe.
   - (A) revolved
   - (B) resolved
   - (C) fluctuated
   - (D) remembered

18. We slept in hostels and cooked our meals in _____ kitchens.
   - (F) capricious
   - (G) coexist
   - (H) communal
   - (J) company

19. Mei's guidebook had _____ descriptions of famous attractions.
   - (A) succinct
   - (B) compatible
   - (C) blatant
   - (D) curt

20. We got lost, arriving at Blackheath Castle by a _____ route.
   - (F) direct
   - (G) linear
   - (H) picturesque
   - (J) roundabout

For numbers 21–24, read each item. Choose the word that correctly completes both sentences.

21. We set up our camp near the _____ of the mountain.
    The runner rounded first _____ and headed for second.
   - (A) foot
   - (B) base
   - (C) home
   - (D) crest

22. We can only _____ corn when the field dries out.
    We visited a bottling _____.
   - (F) harvest
   - (G) pick
   - (H) factory
   - (J) plant

23. The teacher asked her students to openly _____ their opinions.
    The Deerfield Zepher is an _____ commuter that makes only one stop.
   - (A) express
   - (B) fast
   - (C) shout
   - (D) open

24. Tami couldn't clean the _____ in the collar of her shirt.
    You can win a prize if you can _____ the bell.
   - (F) dirt
   - (G) ring
   - (H) shoot
   - (J) capture

GO ON

READING PRACTICE TEST
Part 1: Vocabulary (cont.)

For numbers 25–32, read the paragraph. Find the word below the paragraph that fits best in each numbered blank.

To travel across the desert, there is one **(25)**_____ rule. Make your trip with water! The desert is not always flat. There are sometimes **(26)**_____. Because the desert is so dry, the plants do not **(27)**_____ many flowers. The climate of the desert is dry and never **(28)**_____. A footprint in the desert would quickly **(29)**_____ in the blowing sand. There's not just one kind of cactus, but **(30)**_____ species of cactuses living in the desert. Wearing sunglasses is a good **(31)**_____ if you are in the desert sun. The desert sun is very **(32)**_____.

25.
- (A) absolute
- (B) nearly
- (C) unknown
- (D) untested

26.
- (F) problems
- (G) transients
- (H) tables
- (J) dunes

27.
- (A) handle
- (B) harvest
- (C) bear
- (D) clip

28.
- (F) arid
- (G) hot
- (H) muggy
- (J) protected

29.
- (A) appear
- (B) vast
- (C) compare
- (D) vanish

30.
- (F) singular
- (G) diverse
- (H) absolute
- (J) twelve

31.
- (A) map
- (B) precaution
- (C) complete
- (D) condition

32.
- (F) dry
- (G) insulated
- (H) intense
- (J) common

STOP

READING PRACTICE TEST

● **Part 2: Comprehension**

Directions: Read each article in this section carefully. Then choose the correct answer and fill in the circle that corresponds to that choice.

Example

> Do you know how television works? The picture taken by the camera is turned into an electronic pulse that is broadcast into the air. The receiver in your television picks up the signal and turns it into the picture you see on the screen.

A. **In this passage, the word *broadcast* means**

- Ⓐ received
- Ⓑ sent
- Ⓒ created
- Ⓓ weakened

Giant of the Forest

Every part of the country has a special tree that is native to that region. On the northwest coast of the United States, that special tree is called the redwood. These tall, reddish-brown trees grow in beautiful forests, usually near the ocean. Redwood trees need a great deal of moisture, and being near the ocean provides them with ample exposure to rain and fog.

Redwoods grow to be very old, with some living for hundreds of years. Scientists know the age of any of these trees by looking at its growth rings. If a redwood tree is cut crossways, you can see these rings. A ring is formed for each year of a tree's life. Researchers study redwood tree rings not only to learn the age of the tree, but to learn what the climate and environmental conditions were like in the forest as the tree was growing.

Redwood trees are ecologically important. Most of them are protected in state and national parks and won't be cut for lumber.

Redwoods exist in ecosystems that depend on trees for survival. The branches and leaves of redwoods collect moisture that feeds the tree and sustains the forest life below it. Many different species of flowers, plants, insects, and vertebrate animals coexist with redwoods. It is not uncommon to see deer, birds, slugs, ferns, and flowers when walking through a dense redwood forest.

Unlike most other trees, redwoods are fairly resistant to insects and floods. Redwood trees are also fire-resistant to some extent, and even depend on periodic, low-intensity fires to clear away ground cover and encourage new growth. Most redwoods that die naturally die from being knocked over by high winds.

Even after a redwood tree falls, it has an important role to play in the forest. It can take hundreds of years for a dead redwood log to decompose completely. During that time, the log is home to many animals and various types of fungus. The impact these creatures have on the log helps it to break down and become part of the soil where seeds will start new life.

GO ON

48 978-1-62057-600-7 *Spectrum Test Practice 8*

READING: PRACTICE TEST

Part 2: Comprehension (cont.)

1. **This article is mostly about—**

   (A) how a forest grows.

   (B) how to identify forest plants.

   (C) forest animals and birds.

   (D) a unique kind of tree.

2. **The author says that many animals and plants "coexist with redwoods." The word *coexist* probably means—**

   (F) compete for food.

   (G) struggle for life.

   (H) live together.

   (J) have common enemies.

3. **Low-intensity forest fires help redwood forests because—**

   (A) they scare away animals and birds.

   (B) the old undergrowth is burned away.

   (C) they help the trees to decompose faster.

   (D) they turn the tree bark a reddish color.

4. **Choose the sentence that best supports your answer for number 2.**

   (F) A forest always includes animals and plants.

   (G) Without animals, there wouldn't be any trees.

   (H) There is competition between animals and plants.

   (J) The forest is an extremely wild place.

5. **Select the sentence that best summarizes the life cycle of a redwood tree.**

   (A) When a redwood tree dies, the log is always made into lumber.

   (B) Redwoods grow, die, and decompose all within one year.

   (C) A redwood tree dies only when it is knocked over by the wind.

   (D) Redwood trees grow, die, then decompose into the earth.

6. **Which of these facts about the passage helps identify it as a *descriptive passage*?**

   (F) It is written in question-and-answer format.

   (G) It gives steps and teaches a new technique.

   (H) It includes a wide range of information.

   (J) It is about something that is found in nature.

7. **If you wanted to find out more about redwood trees, which of these resources would be most helpful?**

   (A) an encyclopedia

   (B) a college dictionary

   (C) a world atlas

   (D) a United States map

Read carefully. Answer the items on page 47.

A New Favorite Pastime

Baseball is often referred to as America's favorite pastime. Collecting baseball cards is another favorite pastime of Americans, young and old. It's a fun hobby, and for some lucky people it has become a good investment. Baseball cards can be worth a lot of money. Finding a special one can be like discovering buried treasure. For instance, if you found a baseball card with a picture of Honus Wagner of the Pittsburgh Pirates, you would have a card worth as much as $400,000! In 1936, he was one of the first five players inducted into the Baseball Hall of Fame in Cooperstown, New York.

However, not all cards are worth a lot of money. You can buy a card for as little as a penny. Wouldn't it be fun to buy a rookie card for a penny and then sell it ten years later for $10? A "rookie" is a beginning player in either the National or American Leagues. There are rookie cards for each team each year. Just collecting rookie cards is fun. Another excellent idea is to collect all of the players' cards of a new team. Several years from now, your cards will increase in value as these starters are traded to other teams.

Some collectors like to have their cards autographed and some do not. Those that do, don't think having a player sign a card defaces it. Some cards increase in value by having an autograph, and it's fun to meet the players as you get their autograph.

The first cards were printed in 1887 and came in packs of cigarettes with names like "Old Judge," "Gypsy Queen," and "Dogs Head." Soon candy makers began putting them in their packages to sell more candy. Then bubble gum manufacturers included them with packs of gum, and more people began collecting them. Now the cards are sold separately and are no longer free with your gum. The player's picture is on the front of the card, and all of his baseball statistics are on the back, including all of the teams with which he has played.

You can buy, sell, or trade baseball cards in stores, flea markets, auctions, garage sales, and card shows. Sometimes famous players are at stores and card shows to autograph their cards. They usually charge for their signature, but sometimes they will sign free cards and other baseball equipment at the ballpark or other events. Cards are sold individually, in packs of six to 20, or in sets of 132 to 900. A player's card sells for more in his hometown. This is called "above book" price. There are books in stores and libraries that tell you how much each card is worth in general. You can find the books in the library or in card stores. A lot of other stores have baseball cards. You'll see them on convenience store and department store shelves, even at the check-out stand in food markets.

You can usually find a card club to join in your neighborhood or at school. If you don't have one, start your own. You could invite all your friends for a "card party" and organize a swap meet, or you could organize one with your teacher to be held during break time or after school.

GO ON

READING PRACTICE TEST
Part 2: Comprehension (cont.)

8. **The main idea of this selection is —**
   - (F) baseball cards have become larger in size than they were many years ago.
   - (G) collecting baseball cards is a great hobby.
   - (H) it's better to sell cards than to buy them.
   - (J) autographed baseball cards are not worth very much.

9. **Which of these statements is true?**
   - (A) Almost all superstars charge for signing their cards.
   - (B) The first baseball cards were printed in 1877.
   - (C) Baseball cards usually come in a package with bubble gum.
   - (D) All baseball cards increase in value with age.

10. **Which of these conclusions can you draw from reading the passage?**
    - (F) It would be great to own a Honus Wagner baseball card!
    - (G) Everyone loves collecting baseball cards.
    - (H) The older the card, the greater the value.
    - (J) Rookie cards seldom have much value.

11. **Baseball cards of today can be found in all of the following except—**
    - (A) convenience stores.
    - (B) sports card stores.
    - (C) food stores.
    - (D) appliance stores.

12. **The first baseball cards were distributed in —**
    - (F) packs of bubble gum.
    - (G) packs of cigarettes.
    - (H) packs of loose candy pieces.
    - (J) packages of potato chips.

13. **The term "above book" refers to —**
    - (A) secret prices for baseball cards.
    - (B) cards selling for more than their estimated value.
    - (C) prices that are determined by Las Vegas.
    - (D) entire books of baseball cards.

14. **On the backside of each baseball card is usually —**
    - (F) nothing.
    - (G) the current major league standings.
    - (H) the player's statistics at the time it was printed.
    - (J) a schedule of this year's games where the player can be seen.

LANGUAGE: MECHANICS

● Lesson 1: Punctuation

Directions: Mark the space for the punctuation mark that is needed in the sentence. Mark the space for "none" if no more punctuation marks are needed.

Examples

A. Three dogs were chosen for the finals: Mac, Abbey, and Rebound.

- Ⓐ "
- Ⓑ .
- Ⓒ :
- Ⓓ none

B. Andy please come here and help me carry the groceries inside.

- Ⓕ "
- Ⓖ ?
- Ⓗ ,
- Ⓙ none

 Clue Read the sentence. First check the end punctuation. Then check for missing punctuation inside the sentence.

● Practice

1. Amy asked her mother, "Is there some way I can help?"

- Ⓐ ,
- Ⓑ !
- Ⓒ .
- Ⓓ none

2. Andy the phone is for you!

- Ⓕ ,
- Ⓖ .
- Ⓗ ;
- Ⓙ none

3. The snacks were well received by everyone crackers, cheese, fruit, and vegetables.

- Ⓐ .
- Ⓑ :
- Ⓒ ;
- Ⓓ none

4. The pool, I should add, is not figured into the price of the house.

- Ⓕ :
- Ⓖ ;
- Ⓗ ,
- Ⓙ none

5. "Hold on tight" shouted the driver.

- Ⓐ .
- Ⓑ !
- Ⓒ ;
- Ⓓ none

6. "Let's get out of here before the game is over" said Ace.

- Ⓕ ,
- Ⓖ .
- Ⓗ :
- Ⓙ none

GO ON

Name _____ Date_____

LANGUAGE: MECHANICS

● **Lesson 1: Punctuation (cont.)**

For numbers 7–13, read each answer. Fill in the space for the choice that has a punctuation error. If there is no mistake, fill in the fourth answer space.

7. (A) People should be more careful
   (B) when driving their cars in a parking
   (C) garage to avoid hitting others.
   (D) (no mistakes)

8. (F) Cacti, palo verde and mesquite were all
   (G) thriving in the desert despite the lack of rain
   (H) and water from any other source.
   (J) (no mistakes)

9. (A) While the school year is not yet over
   (B) many of the students are already planning
   (C) fun things to do for the summer.
   (D) (no mistakes)

10. (F) CDO High School
    (G) 122 Calle Concordia
    (H) Tucson, AZ 85737
    (J) (no mistakes)

11. (A) Please send me a copy of your most
    (B) recent catalog of summer programs that
    (C) are available for the coming summer
    (D) (no mistakes)

12. (F) I look forward to your visit as
    (G) I have lots of fun things planned for
    (H) us to do.
    (J) (no mistakes)

13. (A) Wittier College
    (B) Benson Pak, IA 60610
    (C) Dear Dr Adams:
    (D) (no mistakes)

For numbers 14–17, read each sentence. Choose the word or words that fit best in the blank and show the correct punctuation.

14. After you finish this _____ I will ask you to go on to the next one.
    (F) assignment Kim
    (G) assignment, Kim:
    (H) assignment, Kim,
    (J) assignment, Kim

15. The _____ face was covered with make-up and sweat.
    (A) actors
    (B) actor's
    (C) actors'
    (D) actors's

16. _____ wondered Jacob as the party continued on.
    (F) "Why did they leave early?"
    (G) "Why did they leave early,"
    (H) "Why did they leave early."
    (J) "Why did they leave early"

17. If you do not bring both your _____ you will not be allowed to participate in the ceremony.
    (A) cap and gown:
    (B) cap and gown,
    (C) cap and gown;
    (D) cap and gown

STOP

LANGUAGE: MECHANICS

● Lesson 2: Pauses and Omissions

Directions: Choose the best answer for each question.

Examples

A. Which sentence contains unnecessary punctuation?

- Ⓐ Out of breath, I yelled, "Wait. . . for me!"
- Ⓑ It was useless—my friends were already several paces ahead.
- Ⓒ I tried to catch up, but Jaden and Naomi were far ahead.
- Ⓓ Well—next time. . . , I will just ride the bus!

B. Which mark would not fit in the blank to indicate a pause?

The book was better than the movie___wasn't it?

- Ⓕ :
- Ⓖ —
- Ⓗ ,
- Ⓙ . . .

---

1. Choose the correct shortened form.

Mikkel and Short Brush, unhurt but shaken by their arboreal flight, rose and fled immediately to tell their master of the strange doings.

- Ⓐ Mikkel and Short Brush. . . rose and fled immediately to tell their master of the strange doings.
- Ⓑ Mikkel and Short Brush, rose and fled immediately to tell their master of the strange doings.
- Ⓒ Mikkel and Short Brush—rose and fled immediately to tell their master of the strange doings.
- Ⓓ Mikkel and Short Brush. . rose and fled immediately to tell their master of the strange doings.

2. Which is punctuated incorrectly?

- Ⓕ I thought and thought, and finally decided to take action.
- Ⓖ I thought and thought—and finally decided to take action.
- Ⓗ I thought and thought and finally decided to take action.
- Ⓙ I thought and thought…and finally decided to take action.

3. Choose the correct shortened form.

I told him that it has been far too long since we have seen each other and that we should meet for lunch.

- Ⓐ I told him…. that we should meet for lunch.
- Ⓑ I told him. . that we should meet for lunch.
- Ⓒ I told him. . . that we should meet for lunch.
- Ⓓ I told him that we should meet for lunch.

STOP

Name _____ Date _____

LANGUAGE: MECHANICS

● **Lesson 3: Capitalization and Punctuation**

Directions: In Example A, mark the space for the answer that shows incorrect punctuation and capitalization. In Example B, mark the space that will correct the underlined words. If the underlined part is correct, mark "Correct as it is."

Examples

A.
- (A) We need to, help each other
- (B) Don't be afraid to stay after dark.
- (C) This shouldn't be too heavy a burden.
- (D) We can't paint the table until it's dry.

B. If people **care enough, we** can win.
- (F) care enough. We
- (G) care enough we,
- (H) care enough; we
- (J) correct as it is

 Clue If you are not sure which answer is correct, take your best guess. Eliminate answer choices you know are wrong.

● **Practice**

For numbers 1–2, mark the space of the choice that is correct as written. For numbers 3–6, mark the choice that corresponds to the correction of the underlined words.

1.
- (A) Stuart said in disbelief, "he is juggling eight flaming swords."
- (B) "I wonder," puzzled Rose, "Why he doesn't fall from the high wire."
- (C) Mark said, "They must have trained for years to be so good."
- (D) "Watching the trapeze artists, said Rachel, makes me nervous."

2.
- (F) The meeting; will be on Tuesday.
- (G) Gina is president. Until the next election.
- (H) Everyone, at the meeting, is a member.
- (J) If you are late, we'll start without you.

3. We **arent** ready to leave.
- (A) arent'
- (B) are'nt
- (C) aren't
- (D) correct as it is

4. **Rabbits, cats, and squirrels** have four legs.
- (F) Rabbits. Cats, and squirrels
- (G) Rabbits, cats and humans
- (H) Rabbits, cats and, squirrels
- (J) correct as it is

5. **Hurry**
- (A) Hurry!
- (B) Hurry.
- (C) Hurry;
- (D) correct as it is

6. **The balls and tees** were in the golf bag.
- (F) balls, and tees
- (G) balls and, tees
- (H) balls, and, tees
- (J) correct as it is

 GO ON

LANGUAGE: MECHANICS

● Lesson 3: Capitalization and Punctuation (cont.)

For numbers 7–14, read the paragraph and the underlined parts. Choose the answer that shows the best capitalization and punctuation for each part.

Director of Subscription Services

Hikers & Campers
(7) <u>p.o. box 2326</u>
(8) <u>Chicago, Illinois, 60613</u>

Dear Director:
I have not received the last two issues of Hikers & Campers magazine. I request that you extend my **(9)** <u>current subscription,</u> for two months to make up for the two issues I missed. I would appreciate your help in solving this problem.
(10) <u>sincerely:</u>
Tomas Fisher

7. (A) P.O. Box, 2326
    (B) P.O. box 2326
    (C) P.O. Box 2326
    (D) correct as it is

8. (F) Chicago, Illinois 60613
    (G) Chicago Illinois 60613
    (H) Chicago Illinois, 60613
    (J) correct as it is

9. (A) current, subscription
    (B) current, subscription,
    (C) current subscription
    (D) correct as it is

10. (F) Sincerely,
    (G) sincerely;
    (H) Sincerely
    (J) correct as it is

Read the passage below and correct numbers 11–15 by making the choice that will correctly punctuate the underlined words.

One of the newest ways of keeping a house warm is radiant **(11)** <u>heating coils</u> of plastic tubing are built into the floor or slab of the house. When it becomes necessary to heat the **(12)** <u>house hot</u> water is forced through the tubing. The floor becomes warm, and because heat rises, so does the air in the rest of **(13)** <u>the house.</u> It is an efficient heating **(14)** <u>system. That</u> is becoming more and more popular.

11. (A) heating, coils
    (B) heating. Coils
    (C) heating: Coils
    (D) correct as it is

12. (F) house, hot
    (G) house. Hot
    (H) House. Hot
    (J) correct as it is

13. (A) the house, it
    (B) the House, it
    (C) the house; it
    (D) correct as it is

14. (F) system, that
    (G) system; that
    (H) system that
    (J) correct as it is

GO ON

Name _____   Date _____

● Lesson 3: Capitalization and Punctuation (cont.)

Read each sentence. Decide which word that is not capitalized should be capitalized. Fill in the circle that corresponds to the incorrect part of the sentence. If there are no errors, mark "correct as is."

15. In april, the mayor will run again for office.
- Ⓐ In april
- Ⓑ the mayor
- Ⓒ will run again for office.
- Ⓓ correct as is

16. my sister and I went to the movie.
- Ⓕ my sister
- Ⓖ and I
- Ⓗ went to the movie.
- Ⓙ correct as is

17. Have you seen any movies by steven Spielberg?
- Ⓐ Have you
- Ⓑ seen any movies
- Ⓒ by steven Spielberg?
- Ⓓ correct as is

18. The atlantic Ocean is the second largest ocean in the world.
- Ⓕ The atlantic
- Ⓖ Ocean is the second largest
- Ⓗ in the world.
- Ⓙ correct as it

19. the street was recently resurfaced with asphalt.
- Ⓐ the
- Ⓑ street was recently resurfaced
- Ⓒ with asphalt.
- Ⓓ correct as it

20. In venice, the streets are canals.
- Ⓕ In venice,
- Ⓖ the streets
- Ⓗ are canals.
- Ⓙ correct as is

21. Benjamin franklin once said, "a penny saved is a penny earned."
- Ⓐ Benjamin franklin once said, "a
- Ⓑ penny saved
- Ⓒ is a penny earned."
- Ⓓ correct as is

22. Black beauty is a story about a horse.
- Ⓕ Black beauty
- Ⓖ is a story
- Ⓗ about a horse.
- Ⓙ correct as is

23. Many homes in the desert have swimming pools.
- Ⓐ Many homes
- Ⓑ in the desert
- Ⓒ have swimming pools.
- Ⓓ correct as is

24. Those who attended the elks dance seemed to enjoy themselves very much.
- Ⓕ Those who attended the elks
- Ⓖ dance
- Ⓗ seemed to enjoy themselves very much.
- Ⓙ correct as is

Name _____ Date _____

LANGUAGE: MECHANICS
SAMPLE TEST

Directions: Fill in the answer choice for the punctuation that is needed in the sentence. If no punctuation is needed, fill in the answer choice for "none."

Example

A. "We must try harder" yelled the coach at his young team during the halftime intermission.

   (A) ,
   (B) .
   (C) !
   (D) none

---

1. **Some Canadians speak both English and French.**

   (A) ,
   (B) .
   (C) !
   (D) none

2. **Wendy can you help me to move this picture?**

   (F) ,
   (G) .
   (H) ?
   (J) none

3. **In school she played studied and sometimes went out on dates.**

   (A) ,
   (B) .
   (C) ?
   (D) none

4. **Jonathan, will you please try to be home in time for dinner**

   (F) ,
   (G) .
   (H) ?
   (J) none

For numbers 5–7 read each answer. Fill in the space of the sentence with correct punctuation.

5. (A) The alarm clock rang at 7:15 A.M.
   (B) I stayed in bed, until 7:30 A.M.
   (C) At 8:15 A.M. I caught the school bus?
   (D) The alarm rang, again at 7:15 P.M.

6. (F) Corn is grown in Indiana, Iowa, and Illinois.
   (G) Potatoes are products of Idaho Maine, and Long Island.
   (H) Oranges are a major crop in California Florida and Texas.
   (J) Wheat is a major crop in Kansas, over Nebraska

7. (A) Tenth St
   (B) Maple Ave
   (C) Ash Dr.
   (D) Eagle Peak Dr

GO ON

978-1-62057-600-7 *Spectrum Test Practice 8*

LANGUAGE: MECHANICS
SAMPLE TEST (cont.)

For numbers 8 and 9 choose the word or words that best fit the blank and show the correct punctuation.

8. Matt, _____ received a perfect score on his math test.
   - (F) not Mike,
   - (G) not Mike
   - (H) not Mike:
   - (J) not, Mike

9. Please turn on the air conditioner _____ it's 85 degrees in here!
   - (A) because,
   - (B) because:
   - (C) because
   - (D) because;

For numbers 10–13, read each group of sentences. Find the one that is written correctly and shows the correct capitalization and punctuation.

10.
   - (F) Let's move away from here before we get wet,
   - (G) The new sofa is now in the garage?
   - (H) Do you realize that the front door is open?
   - (J) The hammer and Nails aren't where you said they should be.

11.
   - (A) Disneyland, is visited by many tourists from other Countries.
   - (B) If you visit venice italy, be sure to ride on a gondola.
   - (C) If you go to the County fair, be sure you take plenty of money.
   - (D) What time of day do you think we should go to the polls?

12.
   - (F) I was late for class, but everyone else was on time.
   - (G) Randy and Angie, arrived yesterday.
   - (H) The suitcases are packed, and are in the trunk of the car.
   - (J) Summer can be fun but, only if you plan it right.

13.
   - (A) Courtney reminded Garrett, "That he promised to help."
   - (B) We should buy some fruit trees, and plant them in the backyard" suggested Lillian.
   - (C) "The city council has given us permission, added Robert.
   - (D) "Did you remember to bring your rocket?" asked Tim.

For numbers 14–15, read the passage. Find the answer choice that shows the correct capitalization and punctuation for the underlined part.

"Are you sure this is the right **(14)** pattern?" asked Carolyn. She looked at the tiles the **(15)** carpenter's had already completed and then at the sample.

14.
   - (F) pattern," asked
   - (G) pattern, "Asked
   - (H) pattern asked"
   - (J) correct as it is

15.
   - (A) carpenters had
   - (B) carpenters' had
   - (C) carpenters, had
   - (D) correct as it is

STOP

LANGUAGE: EXPRESSION

● Lesson 4: Usage

Directions: Read each sentence. Find the word or phrase that best completes the sentence.

Examples

A. Everyone _____ to be first in line for the movie.
- (A) wanting
- (B) will wants
- (C) want
- (D) wants

B. As we had hoped, the magic trick worked _____.
- (F) perfect
- (G) perfectly
- (H) more perfect
- (J) most perfectly

 Clue If you are not sure which answer is correct, take your best guess. Say each answer choice to yourself or try each answer in the blank and say the completed sentence to yourself.

● Practice

For numbers 1–3, choose the word or phrase that best completes the sentence.

1. This is the garden _____ Angie planted last spring.
   - (A) who
   - (B) that
   - (C) them
   - (D) where

2. Everything you need is on the table, so please make _____ sandwiches.
   - (F) you
   - (G) herself
   - (H) yourself
   - (J) theirselves

3. Open a window so we can get some _____ air in this room.
   - (A) fresh
   - (B) freshly
   - (C) freshest
   - (D) most fresh

For numbers 4–6, choose the answer that is a correctly written sentence.

4. (F) Stop by the store and pick up milk and bread.
   - (G) The street covered with leaves from the trees.
   - (H) Hold the paper, please I'll staple it together.
   - (J) The radio and television from Warner's.

5. (A) This is the earlier bus has arrived.
   - (B) The most best basketball player in the school is Heidi McLain.
   - (C) Very fewest of us had gone water skiing before.
   - (D) A bright light flashed in the sky.

6. (F) When us went home, we found a big surprise.
   - (G) Let's give them some of the corn from our garden.
   - (H) His was not sure when it happened.
   - (J) I couldn't believe it was actually happening to I.

 GO ON

LANGUAGE: EXPRESSION

● Lesson 4: Usage (cont.)

For numbers 7–12, read each answer choice. Fill in the space for the part of the sentence that has a usage error. If there is no mistake, fill in the fourth answer space.

7.
   (A) The end result of the meeting
   (B) was that no decisions were
   (C) made whatsoever!
   (D) no mistakes

8.
   (F) If I followed you around all day
   (G) long, I'm sure I would be wore
   (H) out by the end of the day.
   (J) no mistakes

9.
   (A) Tommy and me always pick the
   (B) hottest time of day to do
   (C) our chores because we love the heat.
   (D) no mistakes

10.
   (F) The grades I got in school were
   (G) certainly okay with me, but my
   (H) parents said they was unacceptable.
   (J) no mistakes

11.
   (A) The fishes you saw in the river
   (B) were catfish, which are great to eat
   (C) but have lots of little bones.
   (D) no mistakes

12.
   (F) Nixon hit his drive very straight,
   (G) but it went too far and carried through
   (H) the fairway and into the rough.
   (J) no mistakes

For numbers 13 and 14, choose the best way to write the underlined part of each sentence. If the underlined part is correct, fill in the fourth answer space.

13. Traffic on the freeway <u>was heavy</u> because the gem show was in town.
   (A) will be heavy
   (B) can be heavy
   (C) is heavy
   (D) no change

14. <u>Whether</u> it is spring, the trees are not yet budding because it's so cold!
   (F) Although
   (G) Because
   (H) Despite
   (J) no change

For numbers 15 and 16, choose the answer that is a correctly written sentence.

15.
   (A) We gave our dog a bath, but we don't get him very clean.
   (B) The principal give trophies to both of the co-captains.
   (C) The sun shine brightly on the waves.
   (D) Cindy tried knocking at the door one more time.

16.
   (F) Pam receive a digital watch for graduation.
   (G) She send us a dozen oranges from Florida as a gift.
   (H) The unhappy crowd showed its distaste for the concert.
   (J) Our class schedules was printed out on the school computer.

GO ON

LANGUAGE: EXPRESSION

● Lesson 4: Usage (cont.)

For numbers 17–20, read the following passage, then choose the best answer for each of the questions that follow.

Perks is a term for rewards. They are what some companies give to their employees for doing a good job. **(17)** An <u>example</u> of perks may involve giving an employee who has done a good job actual products. Or the **(18)** <u>employer</u> may be allowed to leave work early or be given an entire day away from work with pay. The perk may give the employee access to the best parking spot for a month or a financial bonus. Perks, or rewards, for a job well done help make people try harder to succeed.

As you continue to work hard and earn the good grades that will **(19)** <u>naturally</u> follow hard work, you will want to consider how you may choose to reward yourself for such good study skills and commitment.

Not all rewards need to be **(20)** <u>more extravagant</u> or cost money. Rewards can involve simple ideas like a break from doing household chores, being granted an extra hour of television time, being allowed extra time to be with your friends, or even having more telephone or video game privileges.

17. In sentence 2, *example* is best written—
   - (A) Examples
   - (B) Exampler
   - (C) Examplest
   - (D) As it is

18. In sentence 3, *employer* is best written—
   - (F) More the employers
   - (G) employee
   - (H) of the employ
   - (J) As it is

19. In sentence 6, *naturally* is best written—
   - (A) more natural
   - (B) most natural
   - (C) most naturally
   - (D) As it is

20. In sentence 7, *more extravagant* is best written—
   - (F) extravagantler
   - (G) more extravaganter
   - (H) extravagant
   - (J) As it is

STOP

Name _____ Date_____

LANGUAGE: EXPRESSION

● Lesson 5: Using Verbs

Directions: Choose the best answer for each question.

Examples

A. If I were an architect, I would design buildings that utilize solar energy.

In this sentence, *If I were an architect*

- (A) describes a state contrary to fact.
- (B) expresses uncertainty.
- (C) asks a question.
- (D) makes a request.

B. Give me two servings, please.

This sentence

- (F) expresses doubt.
- (G) expresses a demand.
- (H) makes a statement of fact.
- (J) asks a question.

---

1. The flag is flown at half-mast to commemorate important events.

Why is it effective to write this sentence using the passive voice?

- (A) because the writer doesn't know who is flying the flag
- (B) It is not effective.
- (C) because what is happening with the flag is more important than who is flying it
- (D) because who is flying the flag is most important

2. Which asks a question?

- (F) Jamalia wondered whether her new shoes would arrive in time.
- (G) Let's ask our parents if it is okay to plan a birthday party.
- (H) The herd of elephants wandered until they discovered water.
- (J) Is it wrong to want to have one's cake and eat it, too?

3. Which sentence uses a verb in the active voice?

- (A) The queen was crowned in front of an enormous audience.
- (B) Nothing could be heard other than the voices of the officials.
- (C) Several members of the royal family waved to the crowd.
- (D) A memorable day was enjoyed by all who attended.

4. Which uses the active voice to revise the sentence?

During the second half, an illegal time-out was called by the coach.

- (F) An illegal time-out was called by the coach during the second half.
- (G) The coach called an illegal time-out during the second half.
- (H) During the second half, an illegal time-out was called.
- (J) The time-out called during the second half was illegal.

GO ON

LANGUAGE: EXPRESSION

● Lesson 5: Using Verbs (cont.)

5. **Which makes a statement of fact?**

   (A) None of the nearby coffee shops have a wireless connection.

   (B) I wonder if there is another way to access the Internet.

   (C) Follow me so we can look for another place to study.

   (D) Please provide a wireless connection for these coffee shops.

6. **Choose the sentence in which the subject receives the action.**

   (F) The judge ruled in favor of the defendant.

   (G) Tanisha wished she could camp in the woods all summer.

   (H) I enjoy using apps on my phone.

   (J) Several plants are watered in this building daily.

7. **I would go inside if it were to rain.**

   This sentence

   (A) gives a possibility.

   (B) makes a statement of fact.

   (C) asks a question.

   (D) expresses a demand.

8. **Conduct more research to get better results for your science project.**

   This sentence is written in the imperative mood because it

   (F) commands the subject.

   (G) poses a question.

   (H) makes a factual statement.

   (J) exaggerates the truth.

9. **Choose the sentence in which the verb is formed in the correct mood.**

   (A) If I was you, I would bring a sleeping bag.

   (B) My teacher asked that I walks more slowly in the hallway.

   (C) If I spend the night, I must be home by noon tomorrow.

   (D) Corinna knows it is important that she are ready in time.

10. **How many more weeks are left until summer vacation?**

    This sentence is written in the interrogative mood because it

    (F) offers advice.

    (G) exaggerates the truth.

    (H) poses a question.

    (J) makes a factual statement.

STOP

Name _____   Date_____

● **Lesson 6: Verbals**

Directions: Choose the best answer for each question.

Example

A. Basketball players need to practice daily.

In this sentence, *to practice* is

- Ⓐ an adjective describing the noun *players.*
- Ⓑ the object of the verb *need.*
- Ⓒ the subject of the verb *need.*
- Ⓓ an adverb telling how often.

● **Practice**

1. Choose the sentence in which the underlined portion is an infinitive verb.

- Ⓐ <u>Writing interesting ideas is</u> difficult work.
- Ⓑ After I walk <u>to the library</u>, I will meet my friends.
- Ⓒ Carlos, <u>carrying several items at once</u>, needed my help.
- Ⓓ Can you try <u>to understand my point of view</u>?

2. *<u>Having several hobbies is a good way to stay active.</u>* **In this sentence, the underlined portion**

- Ⓕ is the verb.
- Ⓖ modifies the subject.
- Ⓗ is the subject.
- Ⓙ modifies the action.

3. *The person walking across the street attends my school.* **In this sentence, which word does *walking* modify?**

- Ⓐ school
- Ⓑ street
- Ⓒ across
- Ⓓ person

4. *Tools <u>stacked out of reach</u> are not permitted for use.* **The underlined portion**

- Ⓕ functions as a subject.
- Ⓖ modifies an adjective.
- Ⓗ functions as an adjective.
- Ⓙ modifies a verb.

5. *Having completed seventh grade, Aresia is able to help her younger brother with his homework.* **What does *having* modify?**

- Ⓐ seventh grade
- Ⓑ Aresia
- Ⓒ brother
- Ⓓ homework

6. *Running the race with a flourish will not earn you first place.* **In this sentence, *running* is**

- Ⓕ an adverb.
- Ⓖ a verb.
- Ⓗ an infinitive verb.
- Ⓙ a gerund.

LANGUAGE: EXPRESSION

● Lesson 7: Sentences

Directions: Read the directions for each section. Fill in the circle for the answer you think is correct.

Examples

Choose the simple subject of the sentence.

A.   The **(A)** hurricane left **(B)** people **(C)** without **(D)** homes.

(A) hurricane
(B) people
(C) without
(D) homes

Choose the simple predicate (verb) of the sentence.

B.   The barge **(F)** traveled **(G)** down the **(H)** river at a very slow **(J)** speed.

(F) traveled
(G) down
(H) river
(J) speed

 Clue Stay with your first answer choice. You should change an answer only if you are sure the one you chose is wrong.

● Practice

For numbers 1–3, find the simple subject and fill in the circle that corresponds to that choice.

1.   The **(A)** detective held the **(B)** suspect in **(C)** custody because of the **(D)** evidence he had found.

(A) detective
(B) suspect
(C) custody
(D) evidence

2.   The **(F)** finalists in the chess **(G)** tournament were from **(H)** Arizona and **(J)** California.

(F) finalists
(G) tournament
(H) Arizona
(J) California

3.   After **(A)** breakfast, **(B)** I usually like to take a **(C)** walk on the **(D)** beach.

(A) breakfast
(B) I
(C) walk
(D) beach

For numbers 4–6, find the underlined part that is the simple predicate (verb) of the sentence.

4.   A **(F)** huge **(G)** stain **(H)** ruined the **(J)** beauty of the dress.

(F) huge
(G) stain
(H) ruined
(J) beauty

5.   **(A)** Visitors to the **(B)** cave **(C)** remove **(D)** all gum before entering.

(A) Visitors
(B) cave
(C) remove
(D) gum

6.   **(F)** War Emblem **(G)** became **(H)** the proud **(J)** winner of the Derby.

(F) War Emblem
(G) became
(H) proud
(J) winner

 GO ON

LANGUAGE: EXPRESSION

● **Lesson 7: Sentences (cont.)**

For numbers 7–9, choose the answer that best combines the sentences.

7. **Cable subscribers do get a discount on a digital installation. They must respond by May 15 to get the discount.**

   Ⓐ If you order the discount, you may become a cable subscriber by May 15.

   Ⓑ There is a discount to cable subscribers, but only if they buy a digital installation.

   Ⓒ Cable subscribers can get a discount on a digital installation if they respond by May 15.

   Ⓓ Responding by May 15 will get you a free digital installation.

8. **We visited a TV studio set last week. We watched them record a talk show.**

   Ⓕ We visited a TV studio set last week because we watched a talk show.

   Ⓖ If we watch a live talk show, we can visit the studio last week.

   Ⓗ We visited a TV studio last week and watched them record a talk show.

   Ⓙ While we were watching a talk show, we then went to a TV studio.

9. **I hooked my drive far to the left. It bounced off the fence between the golf course and the homeowners' property. It bounced off his patio and landed in his swimming pool.**

   Ⓐ Because I hooked my drive, it bounced off the golf course, and landed by a fence.

   Ⓑ Because my golf ball went into a swimming pool, it bounced off a fence between the golf course and a property, then hooked.

   Ⓒ Because I hooked my drive far to the left, it bounced off a fence between the course and private property, and landed in the owner's swimming pool.

   Ⓓ Because the ball bounced off the fence, it then hooked and went into the pool.

For numbers 10 and 11, choose the best way of expressing the idea.

10. Ⓕ Having just finished work on the cabin, the contractor stepped back, filled with pride, and admired it.

    Ⓖ Filled with pride, the contractor stepped back and admired the cabin he had just built.

    Ⓗ The contractor was filled with pride, stepping back to admire the cabin he had just built.

    Ⓙ The cabin he had just built filled the contractor with pride, so he stepped back and admired it.

11. Ⓐ Ryan wasn't certain what time the game started, so he called the ticket office.

    Ⓑ Calling the ticket office, Ryan wasn't certain what time the game started.

    Ⓒ Because he called the ticket office, Ryan wasn't sure what time the game started.

    Ⓓ Although he wasn't sure what time the game started, Ryan called the ticket office.

GO ON

LANGUAGE: EXPRESSION

● **Lesson 7: Sentences (cont.)**

Read the following passage and then choose the best answer for each question that follows.

(1) A hurricane is a form of a cyclone, a tornado is another. (2) A cyclone is a region that is surrounded by a rotating wind system. (3) But the characteristics of each differ greatly. (4) A hurricane is like a huge machine. (5) It keeps the planet's temperature in balance by moving hot air from the tropics into the middle latitudes. (6) Meteorologists study tropical storms and general weather patterns. (7) They develop an understanding of hurricanes. (8) They predict their formation, duration, and path. (9) A tornado is like a concentrated hurricane that forms over land. (10) Reach speeds twice that of a hurricane's

12. Which of these sentences is a run-on sentence?
(F) 1
(G) 4
(H) 7
(J) 8

13. How can sentences 4 and 5 best be combined without changing their meaning?
(A) A hurricane is like a huge machine that keeps the planet's temperature in balance by moving hot air from the tropics into the middle latitudes.
(B) If a hurricane is a huge machine, it can keep the hot air moving out of the tropics.
(C) The planet's temperature is balanced because by moving hot air, the hurricane is a machine.
(D) A huge machine called a hurricane moves hot air into the tropics from the middle latitudes, making it balanced.

14. How can sentences 6 and 7 be made better?
(F) Meteorologists study hurricanes and they understand hurricane weather systems.
(G) By studying tropical storms and general weather patterns, meteorologists have developed an understanding of hurricanes.
(H) Because meteorologists study hurricanes, weather patterns develop their understanding of how they happen.
(J) Meteorologists study hurricane weather systems and should understand their development.

15. Which of these is not a sentence?
(A) 2
(B) 4
(C) 6
(D) 10

STOP

Name _____ Date_____

LANGUAGE: EXPRESSION

● Lesson 8: Paragraphs

Directions: Find the best topic sentence for the example below.

Example

A. _____ They are uncovering what may be the largest fleet of Viking ships ever found. These wooden ships may be more than a thousand years old.

- (A) Viking pirates were most active during the Middle Ages.
- (B) Scientists are digging up history off the coast of Denmark.
- (C) The Vikings were pirates who lived in Norway, Sweden, and Denmark.
- (D) The ships are being brought up piece by piece from the bottom of the sea.

 Clue Remember, a paragraph should focus on one idea. The correct answer is the one that fits best with the rest of the paragraph.

● Practice

Read the paragraph below. Then find the best topic sentence for that paragraph from the choices following the paragraph.

1. _____ Abraham Lincoln learned to live with the many nicknames he was given. Those nicknames included Honest Abe and the Rail Splitter. Most of them he accepted in good humor, but he did not like the name Ape, which referred to his gangly appearance.

- (A) The nicknames of famous Presidents were given by their close friends.
- (B) Abraham Lincoln was arguably the best President ever.
- (C) Nicknames are signs of a President's popularity.
- (D) Like it or not, many of our Presidents were not always addressed by their given name.

Find the answer choice that best develops the topic sentence below.

2. _____ People who live in the desert often find great relief and joy from a summer thunderstorm.

- (F) The rain in the desert is needed all year long, but especially during the summer months.
- (G) Many people like watching the power of Mother Nature found in a thunderstorm and often just sit back and enjoy.
- (H) While the rain is pelting down on the desert floor, many people begin worrying about the possibility of flash floods.
- (J) The desert is a place of peace and serenity, especially during a thunderstorm.

GO ON

LANGUAGE: EXPRESSION

● **Lesson 8: Paragraphs (cont.)**

For numbers 3 and 4, read the paragraph. Find the sentence that does not belong in the paragraph.

3. **(1)** In the early 1790s, Catherine Littlefield Greene had a brainstorm. **(2)** She found that cotton seeds could be removed mechanically by catching the cotton fibers and letting the seeds fall through. **(3)** Because she was a high society lady, she was not supposed to associate herself with such dirty machines. **(4)** Her life was much more comfortable before she married.

    (A) sentence 1
    (B) sentence 2
    (C) sentence 3
    (D) sentence 4

4. **(1)** Mary Livermore was the wife of a Chicago minister. **(2)** Mary Livermore's work involved establishing over three thousand chapters of the United States Sanitary Commission. **(3)** The organization's success included providing Union soldiers with a continual supply of fresh vegetables. **(4)** The vegetables were said to have saved the troops of General Grant from a scurvy epidemic.

    (F) sentence 1
    (G) sentence 2
    (H) sentence 3
    (J) sentence 4

For numbers 5 and 6, read the paragraph. Find the sentence that best fits the blank in the paragraph.

5. The artifacts of the ancient Mayan civilizations were first uncovered in 1839 by John Lloyd Stephens. _____. Scientists and historians flocked to the jungles of southern Mexico and surrounding areas. They were trying to determine who the Mayans were, when their culture thrived, and why it eventually collapsed.

    (A) Most Mayans came originally from South America.
    (B) Word of his discovery spread like wildfire.
    (C) The Mayan culture was very sophisticated for its day.
    (D) Many Mayan mysteries remain unsolved today.

6. Ancient sculptors made many bronze pieces to decorate their temples. The sculptor always began the art by carving a figure out of wax and dipping it into a mixture of clay and water. _____. The sculptor then poured liquid bronze into the mold to complete the final piece.

    (F) Wax cut from the figure could be melted and used again.
    (G) Many of the statues were larger than actual life-size.
    (H) The figure was baked to melt the wax and leave a hollow clay mold.
    (I) Bronze had to be heated to a very hot temperature to melt it down.

GO ON

LANGUAGE: EXPRESSION

● Lesson 8: Paragraphs (cont.)

For numbers 7–9, use the paragraph below to answer the questions.

(1) One of the most fascinating figures on ancient artifacts is that of Kokopelli. (2) Kokopelli is compelling, not only because he is cute and vibrant, but because he is everywhere. (3) Several Native American tribes, including the Hopi, Zuni, Winnebago, and Anasazi, tell stories and depict images of the flute playing, hunch-backed little man. (4) Each tribe's idea of just who Kokopelli was is a little different. (5) Kokopelli T-shirts are very popular in the Southwest.

7. **Choose the best opening sentence to add to this paragraph.**

   Ⓐ Native Americans loved Kokopelli because he played a flute.

   Ⓑ Native Americans chronicled their lives and their myths through the ancient inscriptions and pictographs found on the artifacts of their culture.

   Ⓒ Images of Kokopelli are found on jewelry, key chains, and T-shirts all over the Southwest.

   Ⓓ Southwestern Native Americans worshipped characters like Kokopelli because they loved his music.

8. **Which sentence should be left out of this paragraph?**

   Ⓕ sentence 1

   Ⓖ sentence 2

   Ⓗ sentence 4

   Ⓙ sentence 5

9. **Where is the best place for sentence 4?**

   Ⓐ Where it is now

   Ⓑ Between sentences 1 and 2

   Ⓒ Between sentences 2 and 3

   Ⓓ Before sentence 1

10. **Which of the following would be most appropriate to include in the beginning of a report on the Declaration of Independence?**

   Ⓕ The various parts of the Declaration of Independence fall in a most logical order once you know what the document was all about. It was the combination of a lot of ideas that were generated by some pretty smart guys.

   Ⓖ The original document was written by Thomas Jefferson, but he used the ideas of several of his friends and also the ideas of those who were attending the convention. His ideas are timeless because he worked very late at night to meet the deadline getting the document written.

   Ⓗ The Declaration of Independence is regarded by historians as one of the most beautifully written documents of all time. It became the symbol of freedom for the colonists in their war against England.

   Ⓙ If the Declaration of Independence had been shorter in length, most probably it would have been read by more people.

LANGUAGE: EXPRESSION

● Lesson 8: Paragraphs (cont.)

Read the following passage. Then answer questions 11–14 by choosing the best answer to each question.

(1) Elements of science fiction can be found in stories dating as far back as ancient Babylonia. (2) The Babylonians were not very skilled in athletics. (3) Some early Greek and Roman literature related tales of curious voyages and encounters with strange beings.

(4) The Industrial Revolution gave birth to modern science-fiction themes and styles. (5) Intrigued with the remarkable changes going on around them, novelists began to write about science in earnest. (6) The first specialist in the genre was Jules Verne.

(7) Verne wrote such well-researched and fascinating tales that they became the prototype for science-fiction stories to follow. (8) Many scientists from the past and present have credited his words for motivating them to become involved in their profession.

11. Which sentence should be placed before sentence 1?

- (A) Science-fiction themes are purely for entertainment, and never have any bearing on actual events.
- (B) Science-fiction themes include space and time travel, alien invasions, and crises created by technology gone awry.
- (C) Jules Verne's childhood inspired him to become a writer that few people know about.
- (D) Technological advances have made science fiction almost non-existent today.

12. Which sentence does not belong in the passage?

- (F) sentence 2
- (G) sentence 3
- (H) sentence 5
- (J) sentence 7

13. What supporting information could be added before sentence 6?

- (A) Technology was far down the road, so much of the early techniques lacked any kind of drama.
- (B) Edgar Allen Poe, Mark Twain, and Nathaniel Hawthorne all dabbled in science-fiction writing.
- (C) Had Jules Verne not entered into science-fiction writing, he probably wouldn't have become very famous.
- (D) Research and science fiction have a lot in common as we know today.

14. Which sentence tells us the big reason for the success of Jules Verne?

- (F) sentence 1
- (G) sentence 4
- (H) sentence 6
- (J) sentence 7

Name _____ Date _____

LANGUAGE: EXPRESSION
SAMPLE TEST

Directions: Choose the best answer for each of the following by filling in the circle that corresponds to that answer.

Example

Find the simple subject in the following sentence.

A. The **(A)** anxious **(B)** wives **(C)** awaited the safe return of the **(D)** astronauts.

  (A) anxious
  (B) wives
  (C) awaited
  (D) astronauts

For number 1, choose the word or phrase that best completes the sentence.

1. _____ will be home late for dinner tonight because we must go to the library to work on our presentation.

  (A) I and Chris
  (B) Chris and me
  (C) Chris and I
  (D) Me and Chris

For number 2, choose the answer that is a complete and correctly written sentence.

2. (F) The water makes the grass grow but then we had to mow.
    (G) Our new mower runs much better than the old one.
    (H) I cannot mow the lawn unless someone went to get me some more gas.
    (J) The electric starter makes is more easier to get the mower started.

For numbers 3–5, read each answer choice. Fill in the space for the choice that has a usage error. If there is no mistake, fill in the fourth answer space.

3. (A) We had to place film on the windows
    (B) twice because the first time
    (C) we didn't apply it correctly.
    (D) no mistakes

4. (F) Taxes in our city are very high
    (G) because the city council is trying
    (H) to improve our system of roads.
    (J) no mistakes

5. (A) I wanted to claim the puppy with
    (B) the fluffy head, but someone went and
    (C) claimed her before I arrived.
    (D) no mistakes

For number 6, find the underlined part that is the simple subject of the sentence.

6. This **(F)** time **(G)** I plan to **(H)** throw the ball over the **(J)** fence.

  (F) time
  (G) I
  (H) throw
  (J) fence

GO ON

LANGUAGE: EXPRESSION
SAMPLE TEST (cont.)

For number 7, find the underlined word that is the simple predicate (verb) of the sentence.

7. **(A)** Jamie and her roommate **(B)** jumped into the **(C)** hotel swimming pool at the same **(D)** time.

   (A) Jamie
   (B) jumped
   (C) hotel
   (D) time

For numbers 8–10, choose the answer that best combines the underlined sentences.

8. **The student brought the apples to school. The student gave an apple to each classmate.**

   (F) The student gave apples to his classmates.
   (G) The student brought the apples to school and gave one to each classmate.
   (H) The student brought the apples to school and gave an apple to each classmate.
   (J) The student brought the apples to school because his classmates wanted them.

9. **The Sahara Desert has nearly 100 large oases. An oasis is a place with water.**

   (A) The Sahara Desert has nearly 100 oases, with water.
   (B) The Sahara Desert has nearly 100 large oases—places with water.
   (C) There are nearly 100 large oases of water in the Sahara Desert.
   (D) The Sahara Desert has nearly 100 large places with water, oases.

10. **My mom was sick today. We did not go shopping.**

   (F) Today my mom was sick, and we did not go shopping.
   (G) My mom was sick today so we did not go shopping.
   (H) My mom, today was sick because we did not go shopping.
   (J) My mom was sick, and today we did not go shopping.

For numbers 11 and 12, choose the best way of expressing the idea.

11. (A) The camera you want is not in this store, although they do sell them.
   (B) The store has cameras that the camera store does not want you to buy.
   (C) This store, which has camera, although not the kind you want.
   (D) Although not the kind of camera you really want to buy, the store does have them.

12. (F) The Charters of Freedom are promptly put to bed every night at Washington, D.C.
   (G) Every night at the National Archives in Washington, D.C., the Charters of Freedom are promptly put to bed.
   (H) Every night the Charters of Freedom go to bed promptly in Washington, D.C., when they are told to go.
   (J) Washington, D.C. is the home to both the National Archives and the Charters of Freedom.

GO ON

Name _____ Date_____

Read the paragraph below. Find the best topic sentence for the paragraph.

13. _____ The index is an alphabetical listing of the main topics treated in a book. Subtopics are listed alphabetically under the main topics. The pages on which information can be found are indicated alongside the topic.

   (A) The index to a daily newspaper fills many books.

   (B) Index cards are handy for taking notes from an encyclopedia.

   (C) A good reader knows how to use an index.

   (D) An index is useful for locating specific information in a book.

Read the sentence below. Find the best supporting sentence.

14. **Muscles connected to your skeleton are called voluntary muscles.**

   (F) Muscles always work in pairs so joints can move in different directions.

   (G) The human skeleton contains over two hundred bones. Sixty-four of these are found in the arms and hands.

   (H) This means they are under your direct control. You can move these muscles almost any way you want to.

   (J) Some muscles are not connected to your skeleton. For example, your heart contains muscles, but you cannot control their movement.

Read the paragraph below. Find the sentence that does not belong in the paragraph.

15. **(1)** The initials FDR are among the most famous in all of American history. **(2)** While millions of Americans loved him, some did not like him at all. **(3)** He was born into a wealthy family. **(4)** Franklin Delano Roosevelt was president of the United States longer than any other man.

   (A) sentence 1

   (B) sentence 2

   (C) sentence 3

   (D) sentence 4

Read the paragraph below. Find the sentence that best fits the blank in the paragraph.

16. **When John Parke Custis, Martha Washington's son by her first marriage, died, the Washingtons raised his two youngest children. Just before George and Martha married, Washington legally adopted the girl, but he did not adopt her brother. _____ George Washington Parke Custis (the son Washington did not adopt) began building Arlington House on 1100 acres of land owned by his father. Today that land is Arlington National Cemetery.**

   (F) Washington did not adopt the boy because he thought it might affect his claim to the Custis estate.

   (G) Washington wanted a cemetery.

   (H) If Martha had not died when she did, Arlington National Cemetery would probably have not become a reality.

   (J) George Washington Parke Custis married Mary Lee Fitzhugh in Washington, D.C.

GO ON

LANGUAGE: EXPRESSION
SAMPLE TEST (cont.)

Read the following passage then use it to help you choose the correct answers to questions 17–20.

(1) It was on September 19, 1870, at a campfire in Yellowstone, that the idea of a national park was actually born. (2) While seated around the fire, a group of men discussed what should be done to save forever this outstanding country they had been exploring. (3) Some suggested staking out personal claims, but Cornelius Hedges suggested that Yellowstone's unique beauty should belong to all the people as a national park. (4) Other men thought this was a great idea and pledged their support of the measure before Congress. (5) In 1871 an expedition under Dr. Ferdinand Hayden of the U.S. Geological Society visited Yellowstone. (6) He took with him a photographer named William H. Jackson. (7) Members of Congress found his pictures on their desks when they assembled to debate the establishment of Yellowstone as a park. (8) The impact of Jackson's photographs no doubt played a major role in the future of Yellowstone. (9) A great victory for Dr. Hayden.

17. In sentence 2, <u>save forever</u> is best written—

- (A) preserve
- (B) extend beyond time
- (C) domesticate
- (D) As it is

18. How is sentence 4 best written?

- (F) While other men thought this was also a good idea, they pledged their support of the measure before Congress.
- (G) Congress supported the measure because it was such a good idea of Hedges.
- (H) Because it was such a great idea, Hedges himself thought it should be brought up before Congress.
- (J) As it is

19. Which of these sentences would best follow sentence 6?

- (A) Jackson was a former still life photographer, which is why he was commissioned by Dr. Hayden.
- (B) Most photographers at the time preferred shooting portraits to nature photography.
- (C) Dr. Hayes' instructions to Jackson were to try to catch some wildlife in action.
- (D) Jackson's photographs captured the splendor of the country and the drama of the exploration.

20. Which group of words is not a sentence?

- (F) sentence 2
- (G) sentence 5
- (H) sentence 6
- (J) sentence 9

 978-1-62057-600-7 *Spectrum Test Practice 8*

LANGUAGE: SPELLING

● Lesson 9: Spelling Skills

Directions: Follow the directions for each section. Choose the answer you think is correct.

Examples

Find the word that is spelled correctly and fits best in the blank

A.   What time will be _____ to you?

- (A) acceptible
- (B) acceptable
- (C) accaptable
- (D) acceptabel

B.   Choose the phrase in which the underlined word is not spelled correctly.

- (F) dangerous ride
- (G) small broshure
- (H) important bulletin
- (J) bouquet of flowers

Clue Read the directions carefully. Be sure you know if you are looking for the correctly spelled or incorrectly spelled word.

● Practice

For numbers 1–4, find the word that is spelled correctly and fits best in the blank.

1.   The gas _____ registered empty.
- (A) gage
- (B) geaug
- (C) gauge
- (D) guage

2.   The move was absolutely _____!
- (F) funtastic
- (G) fantactus
- (H) fantasteic
- (J) fantastic

3.   The _____ was heard for miles.
- (A) exploision
- (B) explosen
- (C) explosan
- (D) explosion

4.   She read the poem in an _____ voice.
- (F) expresive
- (G) exprissive
- (H) expressive
- (J) espressive

For numbers 5–7, choose the phrase in which the underlined word is not spelled correctly.

5.
- (A) gasoline monopoly
- (B) multiplication tables
- (C) basic necesity
- (D) art museum

6.
- (F) she wore mocassins
- (G) the murmur of voices
- (H) Greek mythology
- (J) institutions of learning

7.
- (A) investigate the scene
- (B) invasion of the aliens
- (C) a sweet ingredient
- (D) a greade influence

GO ON

LANGUAGE: SPELLING

● Lesson 9: Spelling Skills (cont.)

For numbers 8–10, read each answer. Fill in the space for the choice that has a spelling error. If there is no mistake, fill in the last answer space.

8.
- (F) scissors
- (G) sherrif
- (H) shroud
- (J) (no mistakes)

9.
- (A) steadiest
- (B) scholar
- (C) security
- (D) (no mistakes)

10.
- (F) sargeant
- (G) significant
- (H) specific
- (J) (no mistakes)

For numbers 11–13, read each phrase. One of the underlined words is not spelled correctly for the way it is used in the phrase. Fill in the space for the word that is not spelled correctly.

11.
- (A) breakfast role
- (B) stir the soup
- (C) hand it to Molly
- (D) hop the table

12.
- (F) grove of trees
- (G) angle of ascent
- (H) bread and butter
- (J) cent of victory

13.
- (A) starring role
- (B) scent of flowers
- (C) bred the horses
- (D) vauge response

For numbers 14–17, find the underlined word that is misspelled. If all the words are spelled correctly, mark the space no mistake.

14. Your (F) behavior during the (G) interim was (H) unacceptable. (J) no mistake
- (F) behavior
- (G) interim
- (H) unacceptable
- (J) no mistake

15. The (A) professional baseball player's (B) autograf was (C) authentic. (D) no mistake
- (A) professional
- (B) autograf
- (C) authentic
- (D) no mistake

16. The (F) souviner was quite (G) valuable to the owner, even though the real cost was (H) inexpensive. (J) no mistake
- (F) souviner
- (G) valuable
- (H) inexpensive
- (J) no mistake

17. In (A) physical education the (B) instructor made us try to do a (C) summersault. (D) no mistake
- (A) physical
- (B) instructor
- (C) summersault
- (D) no mistake

STOP

LANGUAGE: SPELLING
SAMPLE TEST

Directions: For A, choose the word that is spelled correctly and fits best in the blank. For B, choose the phrase in which the underlined word is not spelled correctly.

Examples

A.   The _____ landed just outside the city.
- (A) astroide
- (B) asturoid
- (C) asteroid
- (D) astirode

B.
- (F) manipulate the tool
- (G) bisected angle
- (H) impresive drawing
- (J) tall antenna

For numbers 1–6, find the word that is spelled correctly and fits best in the blank.

1.   The _____ inventor made a startling discovery.
- (A) ambitious
- (B) ambishus
- (C) ambitus
- (D) ambichus

2.   He was a _____ runner with the ball.
- (F) versatil
- (G) versatal
- (H) versatile
- (J) vursatul

3.   What is the _____ policy?
- (A) cancelation
- (B) cancellation
- (C) cancelashon
- (D) cancelaton

4.   The _____ was visible in the western sky.
- (F) constelation
- (G) constellation
- (H) constullation
- (J) constilation

5.   She is _____ to her parents.
- (A) indeted
- (B) endeted
- (C) endebted
- (D) indebted

6.   The pain was _____.
- (F) excrusiating
- (G) excrushiating
- (H) excrucieting
- (J) excruciating

For numbers 7–9, read the phrases. Choose the phrase in which the underlined word is **not** spelled correctly.

7.
- (A) discontinued color
- (B) spontaneous combustion
- (C) receptshonist at the desk
- (D) immense building

8.
- (F) incredible journey
- (G) initiate the action
- (H) prosperus engineer
- (J) impatient child

9.
- (A) iliterate student
- (B) gnaw on the bone
- (C) quietest of them all
- (D) latent hostility

GO ON

Name _____   Date_____

LANGUAGE: SPELLING
SAMPLE TEST (cont.)

For numbers 10–12, read each answer. Fill in the space for the choice that has a spelling error. If there is no mistake, fill in the last answer space.

10. (F) calves
     (G) sheaves
     (H) heroes
     (J) no mistakes

11. (A) dispense
     (B) proceded
     (C) tyrant
     (D) no mistakes

12. (F) accidentaly
     (G) inescapable
     (H) concede
     (J) no mistakes

For numbers 13–15, read each phrase. One of the underlined words is not spelled correctly for the way it is used. Fill in the space for the word that is not spelled correctly.

13. (A) immerse in water
     (B) impartial jury
     (C) inconclusive results
     (D) nuetral position

14. (F) ninety two
     (G) optamism class
     (H) recent occurrence
     (J) orchestrate the action

15. (A) apartment complex
     (B) hungry and penniless
     (C) setting a presedent
     (D) perpetual motion

For numbers 16–19, find the underlined part that is misspelled. If all the words are spelled correctly, mark the space no mistake.

16. Two (F) shipments of televisions were (G) physically damaged by (H) vandels. (J) no mistake
     (F) shipments
     (G) physically
     (H) vandels
     (J) no mistake

17. Farmers cannot (A) cultavate their fields because of the (B) recent (C) torrential downpour. (D) no mistake
     (A) cultavate
     (B) recent
     (C) torrential
     (D) no mistake

18. A (F) horrible (G) accident just (H) occurred on the freeway. (J) no mistake
     (F) horrible
     (G) accident
     (H) occurred
     (J) no mistake

19. The (A) personality of our new (B) secretary is (C) charming. (D) no mistake
     (A) personality
     (B) secretary
     (C) charming
     (D) no mistake

STOP

Name _____ Date_____

LANGUAGE: STUDY SKILLS

● Lesson 10: Study Skills

Directions: Follow the directions for each section. Choose the answer you think is correct.

A. Look at the map on the left. Which direction was the Incan culture from the Mayan culture?

- (A) northeast
- (B) northwest
- (C) southeast
- (D) southwest

If you are not sure which answer choice is correct, try this strategy. Read the question, look at the illustration if there is one, and then look at the answer choices. If necessary, read the question again. Then try to find the right answer. Use this graph to answer numbers 1–4.

● Practice

Rainy Days

Average Number of Rainy Days in Miami, Florida

1. Which month of the year has the most rainy days?
   - (A) June
   - (B) July
   - (C) September
   - (D) October

2. Which month would you go to Miami if you wanted to avoid rainy days?
   - (F) January
   - (G) February
   - (H) November
   - (J) December

3. In which three-month period does most of the rain fall in Miami, Florida?
   - (A) April, May, June
   - (B) May, June, July
   - (C) July, August, September
   - (D) August, September, October

4. What is the range between the month with the least number of rainy days and the month with the most rainy days?
   - (F) 20
   - (G) 15
   - (H) 12
   - (J) 10

GO ON

LANGUAGE: STUDY SKILLS

● Lesson 10: Study Skills (cont.)

Use the table to answer questions 5–10.

Cost of Making Money

Denomination	Cost
$1 bill	3 cents
Half-dollar	7.8 cents
Quarter	3.7 cents
Dime	1.7 cents
Nickel	2.9 cents
Penny	0.8 cents

5. **Which denomination costs the least to make?**

   (A) penny
   (B) nickel
   (C) dime
   (D) $1 bill

6. **Which denomination is the most expensive to produce?**

   (F) quarter
   (G) half-dollar
   (H) dollar bill
   (J) nickel

7. **A nickel weighs approximately 5 grams. Which is closest to the cost per gram of making a nickel?**

   (A) slightly less than a penny
   (B) slightly more than a penny
   (C) slightly more than a half-cent
   (D) slightly less than a half-cent

8. **The average life of a $1.00 bill is 18 months. How many years does it take for the replacement cost to equal the value of $1?**

   (F) approximately 10 years
   (G) approximately 20 years
   (H) approximately 50 years
   (J) approximately 70 years

9. **The cost of making a $1 bill is what percent of its actual value?**

   (A) 3%
   (B) 15%
   (C) 22%
   (D) 31%

10. **The cost of making a half-dollar is approximately what percent of its actual value?**

    (F) 5%
    (G) 16%
    (H) 25%
    (J) 31%

Read each question below. Mark the answer that you think is correct.

11. **Which of the following would <u>not</u> be a good reason to use a dictionary?**

    (A) to find the definition of a word whose meaning you are uncertain of
    (B) to find the pronunciation of a word you are uncertain of
    (C) to find a word that rhymes with a word you've already used
    (D) to find another word you might use in place of this word

12. **Which of the following is <u>not</u> a good rule to follow when taking notes?**

    (F) Be prepared.
    (G) Listen carefully.
    (H) Find a study buddy when class is over to compare notes.
    (J) Write as quickly as you can even if some of your writing becomes difficult to read.

GO ON

LANGUAGE: STUDY SKILLS

● Lesson 10: Study Skills (cont.)

Use the information in the graph below to help you answer questions 13–16.

Minutes Spent on Homework Per Night

(Number of Students vs. Minutes Spent Doing Homework)
- 0–20: 10
- 21–40: 20
- 41–60: 30
- 61–80: 25
- 81+: 15

13. **If there are 100 eighth grade students, what percentage spend 20 minutes or less per night doing homework?**
    - Ⓐ 10%
    - Ⓑ 20%
    - Ⓒ 30%
    - Ⓓ 25%

14. **How many students spend more than 80 minutes per night doing homework?**
    - Ⓕ 40
    - Ⓖ 25
    - Ⓗ 15
    - Ⓙ 10

15. **How many students spend over an hour each evening doing homework?**
    - Ⓐ 50
    - Ⓑ 40
    - Ⓒ 60
    - Ⓓ 70

16. **How many students spend an hour or less each evening doing homework?**
    - Ⓕ 60
    - Ⓖ 40
    - Ⓗ 30
    - Ⓙ 25

17. **Which of the following is a good study skills rule to follow?**
    - Ⓐ Attend class.
    - Ⓑ Take good notes.
    - Ⓒ Join a study group.
    - Ⓓ All of the above are good rules to follow.

18. **Which provides the best environment in which to study?**
    - Ⓕ at home alone in your room
    - Ⓖ with friends outside a shopping mall
    - Ⓗ in the living room watching television
    - Ⓙ anywhere in the house that has the latest pop hits as background music

19. **Setting goals is a good policy in developing good study skills. Which of the following is an example of an immediate goal?**
    - Ⓐ to get at least 85% correct on tomorrow's history test
    - Ⓑ to gather supplies needed for my science fair project
    - Ⓒ to get at least a B this semester in Pre-Algebra
    - Ⓓ to become a commercial airline pilot

20. **Which of these words is not a good word to include in the vocabulary of your study skills?**
    - Ⓕ organized
    - Ⓖ procrastinate
    - Ⓗ committed
    - Ⓙ punctual

STOP

LANGUAGE: STUDY SKILLS
SAMPLE TEST

Directions: Read the question. Mark the answer you think is correct.

Examples

A. Which of these would you most likely find in the index of an English book?

- (A) table of contents
- (B) copyright information
- (C) making inferences and drawing conclusions
- (D) names of authors of test

B. Which would you find in the table of contents of a magazine?

- (F) subscription information
- (G) credits
- (H) listing of the articles and features
- (J) index of advertisers

Study the table of contents from a lifestyle magazine below. Use it to do numbers 1–4.

Contents/Features

27 Special Sections
Datebook
Monthly calendar of events in the southwestern states by Jan Renard.

64 Fashionably on Course
Hit the links in style with a new look from one of the top golf outfitters.

88 Fourth Avenue Street Fair
Ben Swift points out the food fare available as well as a review of many of the wares of the street vendors and entertainment that will be available.

92 Business
Who's New/What's New?
Catch-up column about new faces and places along with info on new products and services.

103 Departments
Out & About
A round-up of some of the area's best places to visit.

120 Spotlight
Previews of several of the month's major events by Barry Long

122 Destination Resorts
Executive editor Scott Hammond takes us to many of the more popular resorts in the Great Southwest, highlighting the amenities of each.

131 Dining Guide
Listing of the most popular restaurants in the Southwest as well as descriptions of the signature dinners of each.

1. Who reviews the restaurants in this month's issue?

- (A) Jan Renard
- (B) Barry Long
- (C) Scott Hammond
- (D) information is not given

2. On what page does the article begin on current golf wear?

- (F) 64
- (G) 88
- (H) 122
- (J) 145

3. On what page might you look to find out what the Fourth Avenue Street fair is all about?

- (A) 64
- (B) 88
- (C) 122
- (D) 168

4. Who has the responsibility of preparing the monthly calendar of events in the Southwest?

- (F) Editor unknown
- (G) Jan Renard
- (H) Ben Dion
- (J) Barry Swift

GO ON

Name _____ Date _____

Look at the time zones map below and answer questions 5–10.

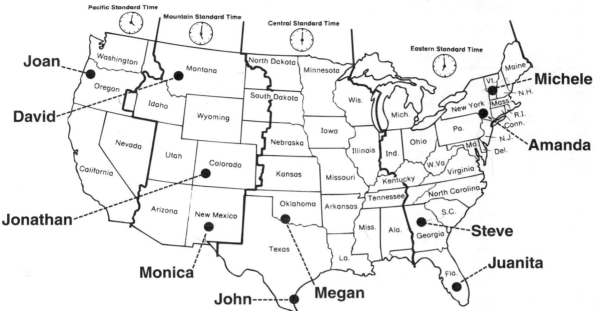

5. If Monica wants to call Juanita at 9:00 P.M., what time should she place the call?

   (A) 8:00 P.M.
   (B) 9:00 P.M.
   (C) 7:00 P.M.
   (D) 10:00 P.M.

6. Michele placed a call to her friend Joan at 10:30 P.M. What time did the call come in to Joan?

   (F) 6:30 P.M.
   (G) 7:30 P.M.
   (H) 8:30 P.M.
   (J) 9:30 P.M.

7. Steve wants to call his girlfriend Megan at 8:45 P.M. What time should he place the call?

   (A) 9:45 P.M.
   (B) 7:45 P.M.
   (C) 8:45 P.M.
   (D) 6:45 P.M.

8. What is the difference in the time between the Pacific Time Zone and the Eastern Time Zone?

   (F) 1 hour
   (G) 2 hours
   (H) 3 hours
   (J) 4 hours

9. If David calls John at 11:45 P.M., what time will it be when John picks up the phone?

   (A) 11:45 P.M.
   (B) 10:45 P.M.
   (C) 12:45 A.M.
   (D) 1:45 A.M.

10. Amanda wants to call her boyfriend Jonathan at 7:00 P.M. What time should she place the call?

    (F) 7:00 P.M.
    (G) 8:00 P.M.
    (H) 9:00 P.M.
    (J) 10:00 P.M.

GO ON

LANGUAGE: STUDY SKILLS
SAMPLE TEST (cont.)

Look at the postal rate changes table below (from the year 2001) to help you correctly answer items 11–15.

Postal Rate Change (1st ounce)

July 6, 1932	3 cents
August 1, 1958	4 cents
January 7, 1963	5 cents
January 7, 1968	6 cents
May 16, 1971	8 cents
March 2, 1974	10 cents
December 31, 1975	13 cents
May 29, 1978	15 cents
March 22, 1981	18 cents
November 1, 1981	20 cents
February 17, 1985	22 cents
April 3, 1988	25 cents
February 3, 1991	29 cents
January 1, 1995	32 cents
January 10, 1999	33 cents
January 1, 2001	34 cents

11. **Which of the following is the standard on which postal rates are based?**
    - (A) 1 ounce
    - (B) 1 pound
    - (C) 1 kilogram
    - (D) unknown

12. **Which of these years represents the least expensive rate increases?**
    - (F) 1975
    - (G) 1985
    - (H) 1999
    - (J) 1991

13. **Which of these years represents the largest increase in postal rates?**
    - (A) 1958
    - (B) 1975
    - (C) 1991
    - (D) 2001

14. **How many postal increases have occurred in taking us from a rate of 3 cents to the rate of 34 cents?**
    - (F) 12
    - (G) 13
    - (H) 14
    - (J) 15

15. **How many times has the U.S. Postal Service raised the postal rate just one cent between 1932 and 2001?**
    - (A) none
    - (B) 4
    - (C) 5
    - (D) 6

16. **Setting goals is a great way to develop better study skills. Which of the following is an example of a long range goal?**
    - (F) Getting through this year
    - (G) Getting through tomorrow's test
    - (H) Becoming a doctor someday
    - (J) Making dinner tonight

17. **Which of the following would be the best source for finding the synonym of a word?**
    - (A) dictionary
    - (B) encyclopedia
    - (C) thesaurus
    - (D) almanac

18. **Which of these sources provides the most recent information on a current topic?**
    - (F) encyclopedia
    - (G) Internet
    - (H) yearbook
    - (J) almanac

STOP

LANGUAGE: WRITING

● Lesson 11: Writing

Directions: On a separate sheet of paper, write a response to each prompt. Include all the parts in the checklists.

1. Write an Argument

Write a letter to the principal of your school. Argue that vending machines at your school should or should not contain soda and other sugary snacks.

Checklist:

Read what you wrote. Did you remember to do the following?

	Yes	No
Introduce your claim.	☐	☐
Clearly express your view and acknowledge opposing views.	☐	☐
Present organized supporting reasons and evidence.	☐	☐
Use words such as *in addition, for example, on the other hand,* and *as a result* to link your claim with reasons.	☐	☐
Use a formal style.	☐	☐
Write a conclusion that supports your argument.	☐	☐

2. Write an Argument

Write an essay making an argument that students your age should or should not be required to wear a uniform to school.

Checklist:

Read what you wrote. Did you remember to do the following?

	Yes	No
Introduce your claim.	☐	☐
Clearly express your view and acknowledge opposing views.	☐	☐
Present organized supporting reasons and evidence.	☐	☐
Use words such as *in addition, for example, on the other hand,* and *as a result* to link your claim with reasons.	☐	☐
Use a formal style.	☐	☐
Write a conclusion that supports your argument.	☐	☐

● Lesson 11: Writing (cont.)

3.   Write to Inform

Write an essay to describe the qualities that make a good friend.

Checklist:

Read what you wrote. Did you remember to do the following?

	Yes	No
Introduce and describe your topic.	☐	☐
Organize information into categories.	☐	☐
Develop each category with facts, examples, and other details.	☐	☐
Use precise language specific to your topic.	☐	☐
Use a formal style.	☐	☐
Give a concluding statement that supports your topic.	☐	☐

4.   Write a Narrative

People sometimes use sayings, such as *you only live once*, to describe how they view life. Do you have a saying that captures the way you view life? Write a personal narrative describing an experience you had that demonstrates your outlook.

Checklist:

Read what you wrote. Did you remember to do the following?

	Yes	No
Capture readers' attention with a memorable opening that introduces important characters.	☐	☐
Organize the sequence of events logically.	☐	☐
Use elements such as dialogue and description to tell the story.	☐	☐
Use transition words to show shifts in the action and settings.	☐	☐
Use precise words and sensory language.	☐	☐
Conclude with a thoughtful ending.	☐	☐

Name _____   Date _____

● **Part 1: Mechanics**

Directions: Fill in the answer choice for the punctuation mark that is needed. Choose "none" if no more punctuation is needed in the sentence.

Example

A. **Did Tom remove his cap when he came in**

  (A) ;
  (B) .
  (C) ?
  (D) none

1. **When you go to the beach you should remember to take sunscreen along.**

  (A) :
  (B) ;
  (C) ,
  (D) none

2. **The basketball team returned to their home city and were greeted by thousands of cheering fans.**

  (F) ;
  (G) :
  (H) ,
  (J) none

3. **How will you ever get that stain out of your shirt**

  (A) ,
  (B) ?
  (C) ;
  (D) none

4. **Uncle Fred my favorite uncle, came to our house for Thanksgiving dinner.**

  (F) :
  (G) ,
  (H) !
  (J) none

For numbers 5–7, read each answer. Fill in the space for the choice that has a punctuation error. If there is no mistake, fill in the fourth answer space.

5. (A) Holmes leaned forward and tried
    (B) to contain his excitement but
    (C) his look gave away his feelings.
    (D) no mistakes

6. (F) I like many foods, but
    (G) these are my favorites
    (H) pizza, ice cream, and cheeseburgers.
    (J) no mistakes

7. (A) Mr. Bentley assembled the
    (B) entire student body outside
    (C) the school for a drill.
    (D) no mistakes

For numbers 8 and 9, read each sentence. Choose the word or words that fit best in the blank and show correct punctuation.

8. **The software will be delivered to you by _____ shipping costs will be free.**

  (F) Friday. Or
  (G) Tuesday: or
  (H) Friday, or
  (J) Friday or,

9. **There were six young colts in the meadow besides _____ were older than I was.**

    (A) me, they

    (B) me? They

    (C) me; they

    (D) me: they

For numbers 10–12, read each answer. Fill in the space for the choice that has a capitalization error. If there is no mistake, fill in the fourth answer space.

10.   (F) Those tournaments are the PGA,

       (G) the masters, the U.S. Open, and

       (H) the British Open.

       (J) no mistakes

11.   (A) On that date, Cal Ripkin, Jr.

       (B) broke Lou Gehrig's record of

       (C) 2,130 consecutive games.

       (D) no mistakes

12.   (F) Arthur Ashe was the first black

       (G) male to reach the final match

       (H) at wimbleton.

       (J) no mistakes

For number 13, read each group of sentences. Find the one that is written correctly and shows correct capitalization and punctuation.

13.   (A) Hundreds of golfers try each year to qualify for the professional tour. Qualifying tournaments are held throughout the nation. In the tournament finals, only 25 cards are issued.

       (B) "I don't know anything about children" said Mr. Craven. "I sent for you today because Mrs. Sowerby said I ought to see you.

       (C) Annie said, "I knew a girl in Marysville who could walk the ridgepole of a roof." "Don't you try it, Annie!" yelled Diana. You will fall and hurt yourself badly."

       (D) The rules and regulations of volleyball are fairly easy to understand. A point or Side Out is awarded for each service. A well played Volleyball game is entertaining to watch.

For numbers 14–16, read the sentence with a blank. Mark the space beside the answer choice that fits best in the blank and has correct capitalization and punctuation.

14. **The coach of the golf team, _____ gives golf balls to all members of the team before each match.**

    (F) Ross Bennet

    (G) Ross Bennet:

    (H) Ross Bennet;

    (J) Ross Bennet,

15. **The tallest peak I can see from my house is _____ It is more than 9000 feet high.**

    (A) mt. Lemmon

    (B) Mt. Lemmon;

    (C) Mt. Lemmon.

    (D) Mt. Lemmon,

16. **The street fair opens on _____ I can't go until Saturday.**

    (F) Friday but

    (G) Friday. But

    (H) Friday, but

    (J) Friday: but

GO ON

LANGUAGE: PRACTICE TEST
Part 1: Mechanics (cont.)

Choose the correct answer for number 17.

17. Which of the following is the best way to begin a friendly letter?

- (A) Dear Cameron,
- (B) Dear Cameron!
- (C) Dear Cameron:
- (D) Dear Cameron;

Following is a letter written by Garrett from scout camp to his parents back home. Use it to complete numbers 18–21.

Dear Mom and Dad,

(1) I'm having a great time here but I still miss both of you lots! **(2)** How is the dog getting along? **(3)** I bet he's spending a lot of time by the door with his tail down. **(4)** Please give him a biscuit for me and mention my name.

(5) We're spending a lot of time swimming in the fox river but I enjoy the canoeing even more! **(6)** We're divided into teams and we're going to have canoe races on Thursday. **(7)** Our team is called the Pirates however I doubt that we will win. **(8)** Our guys really aren't very good at paddling, but we sure do have fun!

(9) The food is okay, but it isn't nearly as good as the way you cook mom. **(10)** I've learned how to pitch a tent and tie some nifty knots. **(11)** I sort of wish you were both here. I'm a little bit homesick. **(12)** I have to get ready for a hike. **(13)** Bye for now.

Love,
Garrett

18. In sentence 1, <u>here but</u> is best written—

- (F) here: but
- (G) here, but
- (H) here; but
- (J) As it is

19. In sentence 5, <u>the fox river but</u> is best written—

- (A) The Fox River, but
- (B) the Fox River, but
- (C) the Fox River; but
- (D) As it is

20. In sentence 7, <u>Pirates however</u> is best written—

- (F) Pirates: however,
- (G) Pirates; however,
- (H) Pirates, however
- (J) As it is

21. In sentence 9, <u>you cook mom</u> is best written—

- (A) You cook, Mom.
- (B) you cook; mom
- (C) you cook, Mom.
- (D) As it is.

STOP

LANGUAGE: PRACTICE TEST

● **Part 2: Expression**

Directions: Find the underlined part that is the simple predicate (verb) of the sentence.

Example

A. In **(A)** <u>time</u> the **(B)** <u>best</u> **(C)** <u>team</u> **(D)** <u>reached</u> the top of the standings.

Ⓐ time

Ⓑ best

Ⓒ team

Ⓓ reached

For number 1, choose the word or phrase that best completes the sentence.

1. The coyote _____ all of the dog food and the scraps of bread that were left for the birds.

Ⓐ eating

Ⓑ were eaten

Ⓒ have eaten

Ⓓ has eaten

For number 2, choose the answer that is a complete and correctly written sentence.

2. Ⓕ If you want we can meet in front of the theater just before the movie begins

Ⓖ We can also meet at, Amy's house which is close to the theater.

Ⓗ We must decide on a plan soon; or go on to a later movie

Ⓙ If we don't decide soon, we'll miss the movie we're planning to see!

For numbers 3–5, read each answer. Fill in the space of the choice that has an error. If there is no mistake, fill in the fourth space.

3. Ⓐ Angie's name was listed near the top

Ⓑ of the program because her last name

Ⓒ starts with the letter B.

Ⓓ no mistakes

4. Ⓕ The Miami Dolphins were unbeaten in the

Ⓖ 1972 season: the first such team in over 30

Ⓗ years to win all of its games.

Ⓙ no mistakes

5. Ⓐ Jose did not appreciate having

Ⓑ anyone leave fingerprints on

Ⓒ his freshly waxed car.

Ⓓ no mistakes

For number 6, find the underlined part that is the simple subject of the sentence.

6. The **(F)** <u>new</u> **(G)** <u>television</u> doesn't seem to **(H)** <u>work</u> **(J)** <u>properly</u>.

Ⓕ new

Ⓖ television

Ⓗ work

Ⓙ properly

For number 7, find the underlined part that is the simple predicate (verb) of the sentence.

7. **(A)** <u>Cacti</u> **(B)** <u>often</u> **(C)** <u>grow</u> in very unusual **(D)** <u>places</u>.

Ⓐ Cacti

Ⓑ often

Ⓒ grow

Ⓓ places

LANGUAGE: PRACTICE TEST
Part 2: Expression (cont.)

For numbers 8–10, choose the answer that best combines the underlined sentences.

8. **My bicycle is in the shed behind our house. I'm sure it has a flat tire.**

    (F) I'm sure it has a flat tire, even though my bicycle is in the shed behind our house.

    (G) While I'm sure it has a flat tire, my bicycle is in the shed behind our house.

    (H) My bicycle is in the shed behind our house, but I'm sure it has a flat tire.

    (J) My bicycle is in the shed behind our house, even if it has a flat tire.

9. **Your friend came to our house yesterday afternoon. Your friend left his sweater in the living room.**

    (A) Your friend, who came to our house yesterday afternoon, left his sweater in the living room.

    (B) Your friend left his sweater in the living room, even though he was here yesterday.

    (C) While your friend was here yesterday, he came to our house and left his sweater.

    (D) Your friend came here and left his sweater, but he was here yesterday afternoon.

10. **Tami is Toni's sister. Tami went to the University of Illinois. The University of Illinois is in Champaign.**

    (F) The University of Illinois, which is in Champaign, which is where

    Tami went, who is Toni's sister.

    (G) Tami, who is Toni's sister, went to Champaign, where the University of Illinois is.

    (H) Toni's sister, Tami, went to the University of Illinois, which is in Champaign.

    (J) The University of Illinois, which is in Champaign, is where Toni's sister Tami went.

For numbers 11 and 12, choose the best way of expressing the idea.

11. (A) While you are in the mall, will you look for the things I've jotted down on this list?

    (B) On this list I have jotted down things while you are at the mall you can get for me.

    (C) At the mall are the things I've jotted down on this list, which I hope you will get for me.

    (D) Although you may go to the mall please pick up the things I've jotted down while you're there.

12. (F) If you don't pass this course, then you should probably take the same course again this summer.

    (G) Eric, this summer you should take the course again if you don't pass it in the spring.

    (H) Eric, if you don't pass this course, Eric, you should probably take it again this summer.

    (J) Eric, you should pass this course, but if you don't then you should take it again in the summer.

GO ON

LANGUAGE: PRACTICE TEST
Part 2: Expression (cont.)

Read the paragraph below. Find the best topic sentence for the paragraph.

13. _____ Carrier pigeons can fly great distances and find their way back home very accurately. Because of these navigational instincts, pigeons have been used even during wars to carry important messages.

   (A) Carrier pigeons love to engage in racing with other pigeons.

   (B) Carrier pigeons have sometimes been used to do important deeds for man.

   (C) Carrier pigeons sometimes are very dirty and people don't like them.

   (D) Large and small pigeons can travel equally fast.

Find the answer choice that best develops the topic sentence.

14. **Many people in the West are finding ways of creating gardens that require very little water.**

   (F) Lawns that require a great deal of water require even more water in dry years. Then you need to mow the grass and fertilize often.

   (G) There are many different kinds of cacti. They make wonderful outdoor plants and are great in gardens.

   (H) Since it's hot and dry in the desert, plants that do well in the East don't do very well in this climate.

   (J) Gardening that makes use of native plants that thrive in a dry climate can be both fun and attractive if designed properly.

Read the paragraph below. Find the sentence that does not belong in the paragraph.

15. **(1)** The names Ben Franklin, George Washington, and Patrick Henry have long been associated with the American Revolution. **(2)** But there were also many women who helped in the cause for freedom of the colonies. **(3)** Molly Pitcher was one of those women. **(4)** While her name sounds funny, you may know her real name.

   (A) Sentence 1

   (B) Sentence 2

   (C) Sentence 3

   (D) Sentence 4

Read the paragraph below. Find the sentence that best fits the blank in the paragraph.

16. The federal government pays for many of the services we enjoy and other programs that are of benefit to many of us. _____ Then the president prepares a budget that shows how much money will be needed for the coming year. Congress then votes on the budget and makes final decisions on how the money will be spent.

   (F) The president looks at the current budget and tries to raise it as much as he can.

   (G) The president tries to determine how much income the government will be receiving from taxes.

   (H) Congress never approves the president's budget the first time.

   (J) Taxes are only raised if the budget requires them to be raised.

LANGUAGE: PRACTICE TEST

● Part 3: Spelling

Directions: For A, find the word that is spelled correctly and fits best in the blank. For B, choose the phrase in which the underlined word is not spelled correctly.

Examples

A. What did the company _____ to you?

   (A) reccomend
   (B) reccommend
   (C) recommend
   (D) recomend

B.
   (F) gas recipt
   (G) proper pronoun
   (H) impartial jury
   (J) preview of the movie

For numbers 1–5, find the word that is spelled correctly and fits best in the blank.

1. He was a _____ citizen.

   (A) prominent
   (B) prominant
   (C) promenent
   (D) promienant

2. The clock was set into _____ motion.

   (F) prepetal
   (G) perputual
   (H) perpetual
   (J) peretull

3. I have been asked to _____ the test.

   (A) monitiore
   (B) monitur
   (C) monitor
   (D) monetor

4. The lights _____ the tree.

   (F) ilumminate
   (G) illuminate
   (H) eluminate
   (J) illuminat

5. It should be an _____ journey.

   (A) inncredible
   (B) incredable
   (C) incredbal
   (D) incredible

For numbers 6–9, read the phrases. Choose the phrase in which the underlined word is not spelled correctly.

6.
   (F) the freedom trail
   (G) in all honesty
   (H) irregulare shape
   (J) launch the year

7.
   (A) leizure time
   (B) sleepy lagoon
   (C) Greek mythology
   (D) satellite service

8.
   (F) fresh samon
   (G) animal scent
   (H) difficult schedule
   (J) steady diet

9.
   (A) shrewd deal
   (B) holiday occasions
   (C) rare opportunity
   (D) nateral foods

GO ON

LANGUAGE: PRACTICE TEST
Part 3: Spelling (cont.)

For numbers 10–12, read each answer. Fill in the space for the choice that has a spelling error. If there is no mistake, fill in the last answer space.

10.
- (F) invention
- (G) invasion
- (H) physican
- (J) no mistakes

11.
- (A) thief
- (B) neither
- (C) leisure
- (D) no mistakes

12.
- (F) mischief
- (G) weird
- (H) heighth
- (J) no mistakes

For numbers 13–15, read each phrase. One of the underlined words is not spelled correctly for the way it is used in the phrase. Fill in the space for the word that is not spelled correctly.

13.
- (A) beige color
- (B) good hygiene
- (C) sealing fan
- (D) excellent grade

14.
- (F) grate golfer
- (G) court brief
- (H) yours truly
- (J) succeed in life

15.
- (A) immature boy
- (B) monthly meetting
- (C) controllable issue
- (D) donkey basketball

For numbers 16–19, find the underlined part that is misspelled. If all words are spelled correctly, mark the space for no mistakes.

16. Courtney's **(F)** opinion was not in **(G)** accord with the **(H)** assembly. **(J)** no mistake
- (F) opinion
- (G) accord
- (H) assembly
- (J) no mistakes

17. The **(A)** legend of the **(B)** beligerent student was **(C)** inaccurate. **(D)** no mistake
- (A) legend
- (B) beligerent
- (C) inaccurate
- (D) no mistakes

18. The **(F)** kitchen **(G)** cabinet came down **(H)** unexpectedly. **(J)** no mistake
- (F) kitchen
- (G) cabinet
- (H) unexpectedly
- (J) no mistakes

19. **(A)** Neither my **(B)** neice nor my **(C)** nephew wanted dinner. **(D)** no mistake
- (A) neither
- (B) neice
- (C) nephew
- (D) no mistakes

STOP

LANGUAGE: PRACTICE TEST

● Part 4: Study Skills

Directions: Study the outline. Then choose the answer you think is correct.

Example

A. **Outline**

Winter Sports

   1. Skiing
   2. Snowboarding
   3. Ski Jumping
   4. _____
   5. Ice hockey

Which of these would fit best in Line 4 of the outline on the left?

   Ⓐ Bowling
   Ⓑ Racquetball
   Ⓒ Curling
   Ⓓ Roller Blading

Study the map on the right that charts the journey of Meriwether Lewis and William Clark as they explored the vast land known as Louisiana. Use the map to do numbers 1–4.

1. The journey of Lewis and Clark was launched at _____.

   Ⓐ Fort Mandan
   Ⓑ Fort Clatsop
   Ⓒ St. Louis
   Ⓓ unknown

2. The river used by Lewis and Clark during the first part of their journey was the _____ River.

   Ⓕ Mississippi
   Ⓖ Platte
   Ⓗ Missouri
   Ⓙ Columbia

3. The direction in which the Lewis and Clark journey began was _____.

   Ⓐ northeast
   Ⓑ northwest
   Ⓒ southwest
   Ⓓ southeast

4. The final leg of their journey in reaching the Pacific Ocean was their trip down the _____ River.

   Ⓕ Mississippi
   Ⓖ Platte
   Ⓗ Missouri
   Ⓙ Columbia

GO ON

Look at the guide words below that appear on a page in a dictionary. Which of these words would be on that page?

5. **marjoram-maroon**
   - (A) monsoon
   - (B) marsupial
   - (C) marmot
   - (D) marquee

Look at the guide words below from this dictionary page. Which of these words would be found on that page?

6. **draw-dredging**
   - (F) driftwood
   - (G) drape
   - (H) dream
   - (J) driver

7. **Which of these is a main heading that includes the other three words?**
   - (A) cats
   - (B) tigers
   - (C) mammals
   - (D) dogs

8. **Which of these might be found in a book chapter entitled "Unusual Hobbies?"**
   - (F) collecting marbles
   - (G) collecting baseball cards
   - (H) collecting stamps
   - (J) collecting salad forks

Here is a map that Jeff drew to show his friends how to get from Huntsville to the observatory. Use the map to do numbers 9 and 10.

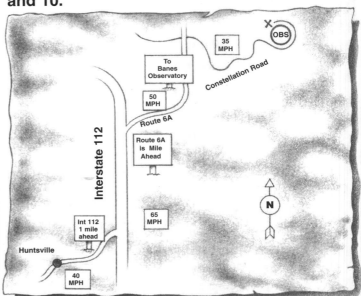

9. **When people are following Jeff's map, which road are they on when they see a sign directing them to their destination?**
   - (A) Huntsdale Road
   - (B) Interstate 112
   - (C) Route 6A
   - (D) Constellation Road

10. **According to your answer for number 9, how fast will they be driving before they make the turn toward their destination?**
    - (F) 40 miles per hour
    - (G) 65 miles per hour
    - (H) 50 miles per hour
    - (J) 35 miles per hour

Name Connie Kelly   Date_____

MATH: CONCEPTS

● Lesson 1: Numeration

Directions: Read and work each problem. Find the correct answer. Fill in the circle that corresponds with your choice.

Examples

A. Which of these numbers comes between 86 and 110?

- (A) 130
- (B) 98
- (C) 79
- (D) 128

B. In which of these problems can the dividend be evenly divided by the divisor?

- (F) $125 \div 9$
- (G) $122 \div 8$
- (H) $126 \div 8$
- (J) $126 \div 9$

 Clue Read each question carefully. Look for key words and numbers that will help you find the answers. Look at each answer choice before you choose the one you think is correct.

● Practice

1. To which value does Arrow D point?

-2   -1   0   +1   +2

- (A) $1\frac{1}{4}$
- (B) $\frac{1}{2}$
- (C) $^-1\frac{1}{4}$
- (D) $^-2\frac{1}{4}$

2. What number should replace the _____ to make the following a true statement?

$$763,812 = \underline{\qquad} + 60,000 + 3,000 + 800 + 10 + 2$$

- (F) 700,000
- (G) 7,000,000
- (H) 700
- (J) 70,000

3. Another way to write 4^5 is

- (A) $4 + 5$
- (B) 4×5
- (C) $5 \times 5 \times 5 \times 5$
- (D) $4 \times 4 \times 4 \times 4 \times 4$

4. What number is 30,000 more than 25,972,043?

- (F) 25,942,043
- (G) 26,002,043
- (H) 26,012,043
- (J) 26,112,043

5. What is the greatest common factor of 52 and 156?

- (A) 84
- (B) 52
- (C) 9
- (D) 90

GO ON

MATH: CONCEPTS

● Lesson 1: Numeration (cont.)

6. Which of the number sentences below is false?

   (F) $^-3 < 1$

   (G) $5 < ^-2$

   (H) $3 > ^-3$

   (J) $^-5 > ^-6$

7. What is the value of the expression below?

   $$(6 + 4)^2 \div 5$$

   (A) 14

   (B) 10

   (C) 18

   (D) 20

8. The value of $\sqrt{39}$ is between

   (F) 5 and 6

   (G) 6 and 7

   (H) 7 and 8

   (J) 3 and 5

9. What is the least number that is divisible by 27 and 81?

   (A) 54

   (B) 81

   (C) 243

   (D) 486

10. What is the prime factorization of 72?

    (F) $2 \times 2 \times 2 \times 3 \times 3$

    (G) $2 \times 3 \times 2 \times 3$

    (H) 6×12

    (J) 9×8

11. $6.12 \times 10^5 =$

    (A) 60,210

    (B) 612

    (C) 6,120,000

    (D) 612,000

12. Which number is between $^-8$ and 8?

    (F) $^-3$

    (G) $^-9$

    (H) $^-15$

    (J) 9

13. Which group of integers is in order from greatest to least?

    (A) $^-3, ^-2, 0, 2, 5$

    (B) $9, 7, 2, 0, ^-3$

    (C) $^-8, ^-5, 0, 10, 13$

    (D) $^-9, ^-5, ^-1, 0, 6$

14. Which of these statements is true?

    (F) $a - b = b - a$

    (G) $a + b = b \div a$

    (H) $a + b = b + a$

    (J) $a + b = b \times a$

15. For graduation, students were seated in rows of 37 each except for the last row which had only 13 students. Which of the following answers could represent the number of students graduating?

    (A) 186

    (B) 309

    (C) 79

    (D) 404

GO ON

MATH: CONCEPTS

● **Lesson 1: Numeration (cont.)**

16. **What is the prime factorization of 98?**
    - (F) 2 x 2 x 2 x 7
    - (G) 2 x 7 x 7 x 7
    - (H) 2 x 7 x 7
    - (J) 3 x 32

17. **Which of these sentences is true?**
    - (A) 5 > 8
    - (B) ⁻2 < ⁻9
    - (C) ⁻2 > ⁻4
    - (D) ⁻4 < ⁻8

18. **Which is another way to write 5 x 5 x 5 x 5?**
    - (F) 5^3
    - (G) 5^4
    - (H) 5^5
    - (J) 25^5

19. **Which group of integers is in order from least to greatest?**
    - (A) 0, 2, 4, ⁻5, 6
    - (B) ⁻2, ⁻1, 0, 2, 4
    - (C) 4, 2, 0, ⁻1, ⁻2
    - (D) ⁻5, ⁻6, ⁻8, ⁻9, ⁻10

20. **What number should replace the blank space to make the following a true statement?**

    1,064,018 = _____ + 60,000 + 4,000 + 10 + 8
    - (F) 64,000
    - (G) 100,000
    - (H) 1,000,000
    - (J) 10,000

21. **Which of these is not a factor of 2,478?**
    - (A) 7
    - (B) 42
    - (C) 32
    - (D) 59

22. **What number is 25,000 less than 28,372,896?**
    - (F) 28,473,086
    - (G) 28,347,896
    - (H) 28,474,086
    - (J) 28,273,896

23. **Solve $\sqrt{196}$**
    - (A) 11
    - (B) 13
    - (C) 14
    - (D) 17

24. **Which number is between ⁻9 and ⁻15?**
    - (F) 8
    - (G) ⁻2
    - (H) ⁻11
    - (J) ⁻17

STOP

MATH: CONCEPTS

● Lesson 2: Number Concepts

Directions: Read and work each problem. Find the correct answer. Fill in the circle that corresponds to your choice.

Examples

A. Four hundred thirty-thousand =

- (A) 40,300
- (B) 4,030
- (C) 430,000
- (D) 4,300,000

B. What is 0.068 rounded to the nearest tenth?

- (F) 0.1
- (G) 0.7
- (H) 0.6
- (J) 0.06

 Clue Be sure the answer space you fill in is the same letter as the answer you think is correct. Key words, numbers, pictures, and figures will help you find the answers.

● Practice

1. Which of these is a prime number?

- (A) 25
- (B) 29
- (C) 33
- (D) 51

2. How much would the value of 63,518 be decreased by replacing the 3 with a 4?

- (F) 100
- (G) 10
- (H) 1,000
- (J) 10,000

3. What number goes in for *x* to make the equation true?

$$2\frac{4}{7} - 1\frac{x}{7} = \frac{5}{7}$$

- (A) 7
- (B) 8
- (C) 6
- (D) 4

4. Which is the best estimate of 62.4 x 58.9?

- (F) 60 x 60
- (G) 65 x 55
- (H) 60 x 50
- (J) 65 x 60

5. Look at the number pattern below. Which number would be next in the pattern?

42, 51.8, 42.9, 52.7, 43.8, _____

- (A) 49.2
- (B) 53.6
- (C) 54.1
- (D) 54.6

GO ON

MATH: CONCEPTS

● **Lesson 2: Number Concepts (cont.)**

6. Make two 5-digit numbers using the digits 2, 5, 6, 9, and 7 exactly once in each number. What are the largest and the smallest numbers you can write?

   F) 97,625 and 25,976
   G) 97,265 and 25,967
   H) 97,652 and 25,679
   J) 94,573 and 24,479

7. What is 9,783,432 rounded to the nearest ten thousand?

   A) 9,770,000
   B) 9,780,000
   C) 9,790,000
   D) 9,790

8. Which of these is equivalent to $7 - (8 - 3)$?

   F) $56 - 21$
   G) $^-1 - 3$
   H) $7 - 5$
   J) $56 + 21$

9. What is the next number in the set of numbers 1, 2, 3, 5, 8, 13?

   A) 7
   B) 5
   C) 8
   D) 21

10. Compare the following products.

    39 x 62 and 93 x 26

    F) same
    G) different
    H) answer unknown
    J) not enough information given

11. What is the next number in the sequence of numbers?

    159.76, 163.72, 156.79, 160.75, 153.82

    A) 157.12
    B) 156.32
    C) 157.78
    D) 156.13

12. Seventy-two members of an astronomy club went on a field trip to Hadler Planetarium. All but three of them paid the $4.00 fee to use the large telescope. Which number sentence shows the total amount paid by all students to use the telescope?

    F) $72 - (3 \times 4)$
    G) $72 (4 - 3)$
    H) $72 \times 4 - 3$
    J) $(72 - 3) \times 4$

13. Which of these is not equal to the others?

    A) 46%
    B) $\frac{46}{100}$
    C) 0.46
    D) 4.6

MATH: CONCEPTS

● Lesson 2: Number Concepts (cont.)

14. Which of the following equations is not equivalent to the other three?

- (F) $x = 28 - 7$
- (G) $7 + x = 28$
- (H) $x - 28 = 7$
- (J) $x + 7 = 28$

15. There are five officers in the 8th grade class. Two are boys and three are girls. If a committee is chosen to include one boy and one girl to represent the school on the all-district council, how many different committees are possible?

- (A) 3
- (B) 5
- (C) 6
- (D) 8

16. If you have 2 pairs of jeans and 5 different T-shirts, how many different outfits do you have by picking a pair of jeans and a T-shirt?

- (F) 7
- (G) 10
- (H) 3
- (J) 12

17. Which of these statements is correct?

- (A) $c + ab = (a + b) - c$
- (B) $ab + cb = b(a + c)$
- (C) $ac + bc = (a + c)b$
- (D) $a - c = b - a$

18. What is the next number in this sequence?

56.07, 57.02, 57.87, 58.62, 59.27

- (F) 59.82
- (G) 59.92
- (H) 57.02
- (J) 59.97

19. How much would the value of 472,868 increase if the 7 were changed to a 9?

- (A) 20,000
- (B) 2,000
- (C) 200,000
- (D) 200

20. Which is equal in value to 27%?

- (F) 2.7
- (G) 0.027
- (H) 0.270%
- (J) 0.27

21. What is 10,287,648 rounded to the nearest ten thousand?

- (A) 10,280,000
- (B) 10,300,000
- (C) 10,290,000
- (D) 10,285,000

STOP

Name _____ Date _____

● Lesson 3: Rational and Irrational Numbers

Directions: Choose the best answer for each question.

Examples

A. Which number is irrational?

- (A) 0.38
- (B) 0.1313313331 . . .
- (C) $0.\overline{3}$
- (D) $\sqrt{\dfrac{30}{7.5}}$

B. Which point best approximates the value of $\sqrt{8}$?

- (F) F
- (G) G
- (H) H
- (J) J

● Practice

1. Which number is greater than π^2?

- (A) 9
- **(B)** 3π
- (C) $\dfrac{99}{10}$
- (D) $\sqrt{90}$

2. Which fraction is equivalent to 0.3125?

- (F) $\dfrac{3}{8}$
- (G) $\dfrac{5}{16}$
- (H) $\dfrac{9}{32}$
- (J) $\dfrac{25}{31}$

3. Which point on the number line shows the value of $\sqrt[3]{9}$?

- (A) A
- (B) B
- **(C)** C
- (D) D

4. Which is the decimal expansion of $\dfrac{4}{7}$?

- (F) $0.\overline{571428}$
- (G) 0.57
- (H) 0.625
- (J) 0.585858. . .

5. Which is a rational number?

- (A) 3.141592 . . .
- (B) $\dfrac{2\pi}{5\pi}$
- (C) $\sqrt{10}$
- (D) $\sqrt[3]{15}$

Name _____   Date_____

MATH: CONCEPTS

● **Lesson 4: Scientific Notation**

Directions: Choose the best answer for each question.

Examples

A. Simplify $(3 \times 10^9) \div (6 \times 10^4)$. What is the result in scientific notation?

- (A) 2×10^5
- (B) 2×10^4
- (C) 5×10^5
- (D) 5×10^4

B. A population of bacteria grew from 4×10^3 to 6×10^5. Approximately how many times did the number of bacteria increase?

- (F) 1.5
- (G) 15
- (H) 150
- (J) 1,500

● **Practice**

1. A city adds 7×10^{-7} kilograms of fluoride to every liter of water. How many kilograms of fluoride does the city add to 100 liters of water?

- (A) 7×10^{-6}
- (B) 7×10^{-5}
- (C) 7×10^{-4}
- (D) 7×10^{-3}

2. Simplify $(5 \times 10^{-3}) \times (8 \times 10^{-9})$. What is the result in scientific notation?

- (F) 4×10^{-6}
- (G) 4×10^{-12}
- (H) 4×10^{-11}
- (J) 4×10^{-9}

3. The distance between the Sun and the dwarf planet Pluto is about 6×10^9 kilometers. The distance between the Sun and Mercury is about 6×10^7 kilometers. Approximately how many times farther from the sun is Pluto than Mercury?

- (A) 10
- (B) 100
- (C) 1,000
- (D) 20

4. Simplify $(9 \times 10^8) \div (6 \times 10^4)$. What is the result in scientific notation?

- (F) 3×10^4
- (G) 3×10^2
- (H) 1.5×10^4
- (J) 1.5×10^2

5. Hong Kong has a population of about 7×10^6 people. The world has a population of about 7×10^9 people. Approximately how many times greater is the population of the world than the population of Hong Kong?

- (A) 1,000
- (B) 10
- (C) 100
- (D) 10,000

Name _____ Date_____

MATH: CONCEPTS

● Lesson 5: Fractions and Decimals

Directions: Read and work each problem. Find the correct answer. Fill in the circle that corresponds to your choice.

Examples

A. $2.10 =$

    Ⓐ $\frac{10}{100}$

    Ⓑ $\frac{21}{100}$

    Ⓒ 21

    Ⓓ $\frac{210}{100}$

B. Which of these is greater than the others?

    Ⓕ two and one fourth

    Ⓖ four fifths

    Ⓗ two and one eighth

    Ⓙ two and four hundredths

 Clue

Pay close attention to the numbers in the problem and in the answer choices. If you misread even one number, you will probably choose the wrong answer. If a problem is too difficult, skip it and come back to it later, if you have time.

● Practice

1. Which decimal gives the best estimate of the amount of the circle below that is shaded?

    Ⓐ 0.125

    Ⓑ 0.375

    Ⓒ 0.500

    Ⓓ 0.600

2. Which of these is less than $\frac{4}{7}$?

    Ⓕ $\frac{1}{2}$

    Ⓖ $\frac{3}{4}$

    Ⓗ $\frac{8}{9}$

    Ⓙ 1

3. What is the reciprocal of $\frac{3}{11}$?

    Ⓐ $\frac{3}{11}$

    Ⓑ $\frac{11}{3}$

    Ⓒ $1 \times \frac{3}{11}$

    Ⓓ $\frac{14}{11}$

4. How would you write 73% as a fraction?

    Ⓕ $\frac{7}{10}$

    Ⓖ $7\frac{3}{10}$

    Ⓗ $\frac{73}{100}$

    Ⓙ 0.73

5. Which of these is another name for three and eleven thousandths?

    Ⓐ 3.11

    Ⓑ 3.110

    Ⓒ 3.0011

    Ⓓ 3.011

 GO ON

● **Lesson 5: Fractions and Decimals (cont.)**

6. **Which of these is the simplest name for $\frac{18}{90}$?**

   Ⓕ $\frac{9}{10}$

   Ⓖ $\frac{3}{14}$

   Ⓗ $\frac{1}{10}$

   Ⓙ $\frac{1}{5}$

7. **What is another name for $3\frac{5}{11}$?**

   Ⓐ $\frac{38}{5}$

   Ⓑ $\frac{33}{5}$

   Ⓒ $\frac{38}{11}$

   Ⓓ $\frac{33}{11}$

8. **What is the least common denominator for $\frac{2}{3}$, $\frac{7}{12}$, and $\frac{29}{36}$?**

   Ⓕ 27

   Ⓖ 72

   Ⓗ 24

   Ⓙ 36

9. **What is 0.038 expressed as a percent?**

   Ⓐ 38%

   Ⓑ 3.8%

   Ⓒ 0.38%

   Ⓓ 0.038%

10. **In this number line, *P* points closest to**

   Ⓕ 0.75

   Ⓖ 0.50

   Ⓗ 0.625

   Ⓙ 0.25

11. **If $\frac{4}{9} = \frac{12}{x}$ then $x =$**

   Ⓐ 27

   Ⓑ 18

   Ⓒ 36

   Ⓓ 45

12. **Which of the following weighs the least?**

   Ⓕ $\frac{1}{8}$ ounce

   Ⓖ $\frac{1}{4}$ ounce

   Ⓗ $\frac{1}{2}$ ounce

   Ⓙ $\frac{3}{4}$ ounce

13. **Which of these is thirty-seven thousandths?**

   Ⓐ 0.0037

   Ⓑ 3700

   Ⓒ 0.37

   Ⓓ 0.037

14. **If you delete the decimal point from 28.023, how does the value of the number change?**

   Ⓕ value would not change

   Ⓖ 10 times greater

   Ⓗ 1,000 times greater

   Ⓙ 100 times greater

   GO ON

MATH: CONCEPTS

● Lesson 5: Fractions and Decimals (cont.)

15. **How would you write 0.7% as a decimal?**
   - (A) 7.00
   - (B) 0.07
   - (C) 0.007
   - (D) 0.7

16. **Which of these decimal equivalents is incorrect?**
   - (F) $\frac{1}{4} = 0.25$
   - (G) $\frac{3}{8} = 0.375$
   - (H) $\frac{1}{8} = 0.367$
   - (J) $\frac{5}{8} = 0.625$

17. **Which of these statements is true?**
   - (A) A fraction is a division problem.
   - (B) The number with the largest value should always appear on the far right.
   - (C) It makes no difference where the decimal place is located.
   - (D) Moving the decimal point one place to the left increases the value of the number.

18. **Which of these decimals has the greatest value?**
   - (F) 17.6171
   - (G) 17.6239
   - (H) 17.6327
   - (J) 17.638

19. **Which of these decimals has the least value?**
   - (A) 0.082
   - (B) 0.0082
   - (C) 0.8
   - (D) 0.802

20. **Which of these statements is incorrect?**
   - (F) The denominator of a fraction tells how many equal parts to divide the whole into.
   - (G) The numerator tells how many of the equal parts are to be counted.
   - (H) A mixed fraction means a number of wholes and a part of one whole.
   - (J) Improper fractions do not make much sense.

21. **Which of these fractions is not equal to $\frac{2}{3}$?**
   - (A) $\frac{18}{27}$
   - (B) $\frac{32}{48}$
   - (C) $\frac{8}{12}$
   - (D) $\frac{64}{72}$

22. **Which of these represents the least value?**
   - (F) $\frac{4}{9}$
   - (G) 22%
   - (H) 0.18
   - (J) 0.436

STOP

Name _____   Date_____

MATH: CONCEPTS

● Lesson 6: Proportional Relationships

Directions: Choose the best answer for each question.

Example

A. The graph shows the relationship between the distance a car travels and the amount of gasoline it uses. How far will the car travel on 1 gallon of gas?

(A) 20 miles

(B) 45 miles

(C) 35 miles

(D) 70 miles

● Practice

1. Which two lines have the same slope?

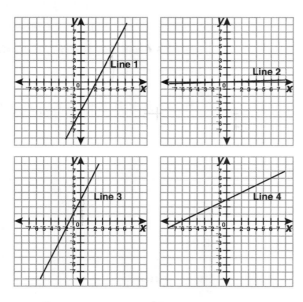

(A) 1 and 2

(B) 1 and 3

(C) 2 and 4

(D) 3 and 4

2. Nick is riding his skateboard. His sister Samantha is running. Nick's distance d in kilometers from home after t hours of skateboarding is given by the equation $d = 8t + 0.5$. Samantha's distance from home is given in the table below.

t	0.2	0.3	0.4	0.5
d	2	3	4	5

Who is traveling at a greater speed, Nick or Samantha? How much faster?

(F) Nick is 2 kilometers per hour faster.

(G) Nick is 6 kilometers per hour faster.

(H) Samantha is 2 kilometers per hour faster.

(J) Samantha is 6 kilometers per hour faster.

STOP

Name _____ Date_____

MATH: CONCEPTS
SAMPLE TEST

Directions: Read each problem. Mark the answer you think is correct.

Examples

A. If you estimate by rounding to whole numbers, what is $6.21 + 9\frac{3}{4}$?

- (A) 6 + 10
- (B) 7 + 9
- (C) 7 + 10
- (D) 6 + 9

B. What is the greatest common factor of 24 and 36?

- (F) 6
- (G) 12
- (H) 18
- (J) 3

---

1. The absolute value of ⁻37 is

- (A) $\sqrt{37}$
- (B) $\frac{1}{37}$
- (C) 37
- (D) 37^2

2. $8 \times 9 - 8 =$

- (F) ⁻72
- (G) 8
- (H) 64
- (J) 80

3. Which of these fractions is closest to 1?

- (A) $\frac{3}{5}$
- (B) $\frac{1}{2}$
- (C) $\frac{2}{3}$
- (D) $\frac{2}{9}$

4. What number completes this number sentence $3 \times$ _____ $= 90 \times 30$?

- (F) 9
- (G) 90
- (H) 300
- (J) 900

5. $9^3 - 84 =$

- (A) 84
- (B) ⁻729
- (C) 81
- (D) 645

6. Which point is closest to $3\frac{3}{4}$ on this number line?

- (F) M
- (G) N
- (H) O
- (J) P

7. Which of these is another way to write 5.2 million?

- (A) 520,000
- (B) 5,002,000
- (C) 5,200,000
- (D) 5,020,000

GO ON

Published by Spectrum. Copyright protected.   978-1-62057-600-7 *Spectrum Test Practice 8*

8. Which of these is another way to write
   700 + 10 + 0.06?

   (F) 70,010.06

   (G)   701.06

   (H)   710.06

   (J)   700.106

9. Which of these is not equal in value to
   the others?

   (A) 7%

   (B) 0.07

   (C) 0.007

   (D) $\frac{7}{100}$

10. Which of these percentages gives the
    best estimate for the amount of the
    circle that is not shaded?

    (F) 50%

    (G) 30%

    (H) 70%

    (J) 90%

11. The drama club set a goal of $1,000
    for its Spring Drama Drive. However,
    they collected $2,460 altogether. What
    percent of its goal did the drama club
    collect?

    (A) 100%

    (B) 246%

    (C) 24.6%

    (D) 2.46%

12. In the numeral 3,860,100, what is the
    value of the 6?

    (F) 6 hundred

    (G) 6 thousand

    (H) 60 thousand

    (J) 6 hundred thousand

13. Which of these is between 0.0036
    and 0.05?

    (A) 0.150

    (B) 0.015

    (C) 0.0018

    (D) 0.501

14. What is another way to write 6^4?

    (F) 6 x 6 x 6

    (G) 6 x 6 x 6 x 6

    (H) 6 x 6 x 6 x 6 x 6

    (J) $\sqrt{6}$

15.   ⁻15
         + 4   (A) ⁻19

                      (B) ⁻11

                      (C) 11

                      (D) 19

16. Which of these numbers is a prime
    number?

    (F) 47

    (G) 49

    (H) 54

    (J) 72

    GO ON

MATH: CONCEPTS
SAMPLE TEST (cont.)

17. Which of these decimals has the greatest value?

 - Ⓐ 7.13
 - Ⓑ 7.24
 - Ⓒ 7.90
 - Ⓓ 7.032

18. Which fraction has the least value?

 - Ⓕ $\frac{3}{5}$
 - Ⓖ $\frac{8}{25}$
 - Ⓗ $\frac{5}{9}$
 - Ⓙ $\frac{7}{8}$

19. Which group of integers goes from greatest to least?

 - Ⓐ ⁻6, ⁻4, 2, 0, 8
 - Ⓑ ⁻3, ⁻5, 0, ⁻4, 2
 - Ⓒ 6, 2, 0, ⁻1, 4
 - Ⓓ 7, 3, 1, ⁻4, ⁻8

20. What is the value of the expression: $25 \div (16 - 11)$?

 - Ⓕ 25
 - Ⓖ 5
 - Ⓗ 15
 - Ⓙ 50

21. Forty-seven boys and fifty-one girls were in the 8th grade class. Which estimate comes closest to the fraction that represents boys in the class?

 - Ⓐ $\frac{3}{4}$
 - Ⓑ $\frac{1}{2}$
 - Ⓒ $\frac{5}{8}$
 - Ⓓ $\frac{7}{8}$

22. Which of these statements is true?

 - Ⓕ $a(b + c) = ab + ac$
 - Ⓖ $ac + b = a(b + c)$
 - Ⓗ $a(b - c) = bc - a$
 - Ⓙ $ab - bc = a(b + c)$

23. Which of these statements is true?

 - Ⓐ $a + b - c = c - a + b$
 - Ⓑ $a \div b = b \div a$
 - Ⓒ $b + c + a = c + a + b$
 - Ⓓ $ba \div c = bc \div a$

24. Which of these statements is not true?

 - Ⓕ $a(b + c) = ab + ac$
 - Ⓖ $a + b + c = c + a + b$
 - Ⓗ $(a \times b) \times c = a \times (b \times c)$
 - Ⓙ $(a - b) - c = a - (b - c)$

STOP

Name _____   Date _____

MATH: COMPUTATION

● **Lesson 7: Whole Numbers**

Directions: Mark the space for the correct answer to each.

Examples

A. 300
    846
  + 197

  Ⓐ 1,433
  Ⓑ 1,343
  Ⓒ 1,822
  Ⓓ 1,386

B. 847
  − 54

  Ⓕ 690
  Ⓖ 793
  Ⓗ 789
  Ⓗ 436

 Clue   **If the answer you find is not one of the answer choices, rework the problem on scratch paper.**

● **Practice**

1. 6,154
  − 1,826

  Ⓐ 4,614
  Ⓑ 4,418
  ● 4,328
  Ⓓ 4,238

5. 658
  − 91

  Ⓐ 749
  ● 567
  Ⓒ 647
  Ⓓ 869

2. 68
  x 29

  ● 1,972
  Ⓖ 1,942
  Ⓗ 1,868
  Ⓙ 1,912

6. 20,002
  x 501

  ● 10,021,002
  Ⓖ 2,042,002
  Ⓗ 14,342,00
  Ⓙ 12,002,002

3. 148)5,328

  Ⓐ 36 R 8
  Ⓑ 36 R 3
  Ⓒ 35 R 2
  ● 36

7. 54)756

  Ⓐ 16
  Ⓑ 24
  Ⓒ 12
  ● 14

4. 866
  + 61

  Ⓕ 627
  ● 927
  Ⓗ 917
  Ⓙ 1017

8. 234
    345
  + 868

  Ⓕ 1,268
  ● 1,447
  Ⓗ 1,362
  Ⓙ 2,447

 GO ON

978-1-62057-600-7 *Spectrum Test Practice 8*

Name _____ Date _____

MATH: COMPUTATION

● Lesson 7: Whole Numbers (cont.)

9. 62⟌23,415
    - (A) 377 R 41
    - (B) 467 R 3
    - (C) 473 R 12
    - (D) 503 R 17

10. 66,577
     x   88
     - (F) 1,418,012
     - (G) 4,136,416
     - (H) 5,476,166
     - (J) 5,858,776

11. 513,420
     − 389,011
     - (A) 214,109
     - (B) 124,409
     - (C) 125,509
     - (D) 105,409

12. 152,897
     + 98,004
     - (F) 250,901
     - (G) 240,901
     - (H) 250,091
     - (J) 240,991

13. 87,211
     − 23,334
     - (A) 73,807
     - (B) 67,007
     - (C) 63,877
     - (D) 43,117

14. 834,521
     + 766,942
     - (F) 1,601,363
     - (G) 1,601,463
     - (H) 2,006,343
     - (J) 3,116,041

15. 679⟌6,004,598
     - (A) 7,635 R101
     - (B) 8,843 R20
     - (C) 8,348 R12
     - (D) 7,536 R110

16. 26,404
     x   42
     - (F) 1,108,968
     - (G) 1,218,412
     - (H) 1,208,968
     - (J) 1,112,408

17. 3,462,018
     − 976,554
     - (A) 1,242,814
     - (B) 2,518,033
     - (C) 2,485,464
     - (D) 2,143,244

STOP

Name _____   Date _____

MATH: COMPUTATION

● Lesson 8: Decimals

Directions: Mark the space for the correct answer to each problem.

Examples

A.	24.342 − 3.797			B.	0.82 + 0.273		
		Ⓐ	22.032			Ⓕ	0.994
		Ⓑ	19.846			Ⓖ	1.122
		Ⓒ	20.545			Ⓗ	1.211
		Ⓓ	19.322			Ⓙ	1.093

 Clue Pay close attention when you are dividing or multiplying decimals. It is easy to make a mistake by misplacing the decimal point.

● Practice

1.	2.8)2.1588			5.	341.050 − 10.623		
		Ⓐ	1.042			Ⓐ	143.227
		●Ⓑ	0.771			Ⓑ	232.127
		Ⓒ	1.141			Ⓒ	330.427
		Ⓓ	2.043			Ⓓ	132.127

2.	22.22 − 9.999			6.	.305).024766		
		●Ⓕ	12.221			Ⓕ	0.0812
		Ⓖ	1.212			Ⓖ	0.1412
		Ⓗ	1.341			Ⓗ	0.812
		Ⓙ	4214			Ⓙ	1.0184

3.	.039 x .009			7.	.3551 x .208		
		Ⓐ	0.351			Ⓐ	0.0492816
		Ⓑ	351			Ⓑ	0.0738608
		Ⓒ	0.00351			Ⓒ	0.0941512
		●Ⓓ	0.000351			Ⓓ	0.0512733

4.	40.092 + 63.98			8.	2.04 3.86 8.45 + 9.99		
		●Ⓕ	104.072			Ⓕ	18.34
		Ⓖ	200.12			Ⓖ	24.18
		Ⓗ	142.212			Ⓗ	24.34
		Ⓙ	186.122			Ⓙ	34.43

 GO ON

978-1-62057-600-7 *Spectrum Test Practice 8*

MATH: COMPUTATION

● Lesson 8: Decimals (cont.)

9.
38.042
93.586
+ 63.108

(A) 1947.36
(B) 19.4736
(C) 194.736
(D) 0.194736

14.
40.092
+ 63.98

(F) 104.072
(G) 106.068
(H) 104.720
(J) 927.550

10.
3.08
x 3.08

(F) 11.4328
(G) 9.4864
(H) 10.4828
(J) 9.3636

15.
.438
x .177

(A) 0.077526
(B) 0.070256
(C) 0.000726
(D) 0.072056

11.
2.005
− .9999

(A) 1.0060
(B) 1.0001
(C) 1.0360
(D) 1.0051

16.
341.050
− 10.623

(F) 330.427
(G) 313.217
(H) 303.401
(J) 331.421

12. .81$\overline{)43.254}$

(F) 534.2
(G) 53.4
(H) 0.5342
(J) 5.342

17.
67.123
+ 62.467

(A) 129.59
(B) 1.04072
(C) 10.4007
(D) 111.122

13. 41.8$\overline{)1185.866}$

(A) 28.37
(B) 38.72
(C) 42.19
(D) 27.46

STOP

MATH: COMPUTATION

● Lesson 9: Percent

Directions: Mark the space for the correct answer to each problem.

Examples

A. What is 20% of 35?
- Ⓐ 700
- Ⓑ 7
- Ⓒ 17
- Ⓓ 4

B. How much is 46% of 4?
- Ⓕ 1.42
- Ⓖ 1.84
- Ⓗ 2.20
- Ⓙ 2.28

Clue Pay close attention to where you place the decimal point in percent problems. It is easy to place it in the wrong place.

● Practice

1. **What is 80% of 40?**
   - 32
   - Ⓑ 320
   - Ⓒ .32
   - Ⓓ 3.20

2. **What percent of 96 is 17.28?**
   - Ⓕ 1.8%
   - Ⓖ 18%
   - Ⓗ 28%
   - Ⓙ 2.8%

3. **66 is what percent of 30?**
   - Ⓐ 11%
   - Ⓑ 20%
   - Ⓒ 120%
   - Ⓓ 220%

4. **What percent of 40 is 14?**
   - Ⓕ 35%
   - Ⓖ 25%
   - Ⓗ 15%
   - Ⓙ 45%

5. **How much is 72% of 6?**
   - Ⓐ 5.04
   - Ⓑ 2.14
   - Ⓒ 4.32
   - Ⓓ 5.85

6. **38% of 45 is how much?**
   - Ⓕ 42.3
   - Ⓖ 28.6
   - Ⓗ 17.1
   - Ⓙ 14.3

7. **How much is 5% of 17?**
   - Ⓐ .94
   - Ⓑ .85
   - Ⓒ 1.4
   - Ⓓ 7.2

8. **How much is 1.5% of 900?**
   - Ⓕ 33.2
   - Ⓖ 13.5
   - Ⓗ 88.9
   - Ⓙ 12.0

GO ON

MATH: COMPUTATION

● Lesson 9: Percent (cont.)

9. 130% of 7 is how much?
   - (A) 7
   - (B) 17.2
   - (C) 9.1
   - (D) 8.0

10. $\frac{3}{4}$ is expressed as
    - (F) 40%
    - (G) 75%
    - (H) 25%
    - (J) 60%

11. .35 is expressed as
    - (A) 35%
    - (B) 3.5%
    - (C) 0.35%
    - (D) 350%

12. Which percent is largest?
    - (F) 2.8%
    - (G) 28%
    - (H) 280%
    - (J) 0.28%

13. How much is 250% of 20?
    - (A) 20
    - (B) 40
    - (C) 50
    - (D) 60

14. How much is 70% of 15?
    - (F) 7.5
    - (G) 8.2
    - (H) 10.5
    - (J) 12.0

15. What percent of 90 is 8.1?
    - (A) 9%
    - (B) 11%
    - (C) 13%
    - (D) 8%

16. 15 out of 48 is about—
    - (F) 0.3%
    - (G) 3%
    - (H) 30%
    - (J) 300%

17. 7 is 140% of about—
    - (A) 50
    - (B) 5
    - (C) 20
    - (D) 2

STOP

MATH COMPUTATION

● **Lesson 10: Fractions and Mixed Numbers**

Directions: Mark the space for the correct answer to each problem.

Examples

A. $\frac{1}{2} + \frac{1}{4} =$

Ⓐ $\frac{1}{6}$

Ⓑ $\frac{1}{5}$

Ⓒ $\frac{3}{4}$

Ⓓ $\frac{2}{6}$

B. $\frac{17}{20} - \frac{3}{5} =$

Ⓕ $\frac{1}{4}$

Ⓖ $\frac{1}{3}$

Ⓗ $\frac{1}{2}$

Ⓙ $\frac{1}{8}$

 Pay close attention when you are dividing fractions. It is easy to make a mistake by forgetting to invert fractions.

● **Practice**

1. $\frac{19}{100} + \frac{6}{10} =$

Ⓐ $\frac{1}{4}$

Ⓑ $\frac{5}{22}$

Ⓒ $\frac{79}{100}$

Ⓓ $\frac{7}{10}$

2. $\frac{21}{25} - \frac{3}{5} =$

Ⓕ $\frac{6}{25}$

Ⓖ $\frac{18}{100}$

Ⓗ $\frac{9}{10}$

Ⓙ $\frac{18}{25}$

3. $\frac{2}{3} \times \frac{4}{5} =$

Ⓐ $\frac{8}{15}$

Ⓑ $\frac{4}{3}$

Ⓒ $\frac{3}{25}$

Ⓓ $\frac{3}{8}$

4. $\frac{5}{18} \div \frac{2}{9} =$

Ⓕ $\frac{4}{5}$

Ⓖ $\frac{3}{5}$

Ⓗ $1\frac{1}{4}$

Ⓙ $4\frac{4}{5}$

5. $\frac{3}{8} \div \frac{4}{5} =$

Ⓐ $\frac{12}{17}$

Ⓑ $\frac{3}{10}$

Ⓒ $\frac{17}{40}$

Ⓓ $\frac{15}{32}$

6. $\frac{15}{32} \times \frac{4}{5} =$

Ⓕ $\frac{19}{37}$

Ⓖ $\frac{75}{110}$

Ⓗ $\frac{19}{29}$

Ⓙ $\frac{3}{8}$

 GO ON

978-1-62057-600-7 *Spectrum Test Practice 8*

MATH COMPUTATION

● Lesson 10: Fractions and Mixed Numbers (cont.)

7. $\frac{5}{6} + \frac{5}{8} =$

   (A) $\frac{3}{7}$

   (B) $1\frac{11}{24}$

   (C) $1\frac{7}{8}$

   (D) $1\frac{3}{8}$

12. $\frac{13}{48} \times 2 =$

   (F) $\frac{4}{9}$

   (G) $\frac{3}{8}$

   (H) $\frac{13}{24}$

   (J) $\frac{5}{13}$

8. $\frac{7}{8} - \frac{3}{12} =$

   (F) $\frac{5}{24}$

   (G) $\frac{5}{8}$

   (H) $\frac{21}{60}$

   (J) $\frac{4}{15}$

13. $\frac{7}{8} \div \frac{7}{8} =$

   (A) $\frac{7}{8}$

   (B) $\frac{8}{7}$

   (C) 1

   (D) $1\frac{1}{8}$

9. $\frac{5}{9} \div \frac{4}{5} =$

   (A) $\frac{20}{14}$

   (B) $\frac{25}{36}$

   (C) $\frac{3}{4}$

   (D) $\frac{5}{8}$

14. $\frac{23}{8} \times \frac{1}{3} =$

   (F) $\frac{23}{24}$

   (G) $\frac{17}{24}$

   (H) $\frac{11}{12}$

   (J) $\frac{3}{11}$

10. $3\frac{1}{4} - 2\frac{3}{4} =$

   (F) $\frac{1}{3}$

   (G) $\frac{3}{8}$

   (H) $\frac{1}{2}$

   (J) $\frac{3}{4}$

15. $1\frac{1}{8} + \frac{3}{4} =$

   (A) $1\frac{1}{3}$

   (B) $1\frac{1}{2}$

   (C) $1\frac{3}{4}$

   (D) $1\frac{7}{8}$

11. $\frac{1}{2} + 1\frac{1}{8} =$

   (A) $1\frac{5}{8}$

   (B) $1\frac{3}{8}$

   (C) $2\frac{1}{2}$

   (D) $2\frac{1}{4}$

16. $3\frac{1}{2} - 3\frac{1}{4} =$

   (F) $\frac{1}{8}$

   (G) $\frac{1}{4}$

   (H) $\frac{3}{4}$

   (J) $\frac{3}{8}$

STOP

Name _____   Date _____

MATH: COMPUTATION
SAMPLE TEST

Directions: Mark the space for the correct answer to each problem.

Examples

A. $20 \overline{)\ 500}$

- (A) 2500
- (B) 250
- (C) 42
- (D) none of these

B. $0.6 \div 0.25 =$

- (F) 2.4
- (G) 24
- (H) 0.2
- (J) none of these

---

1. $3.372 \div 0.6 =$

- (A) 5.620
- (B) 0.562
- (C) 0.056
- (D) 0.006

5. $392 \times 67 =$

- (A) 2626.4
- (B) 26,264
- (C) 26,164
- (D) 5.85

2. $36 + {}^{-}45 =$

- (F) 9
- (G) ${}^{-}9$
- (H) 81
- (J) ${}^{-}81$

6. $25^3 =$

- (F) 625
- (G) 15,625
- (H) 15,675
- (J) none of the above

3. $7(5 - 8) =$

- (A) 21
- (B) ${}^{-}21$
- (C) 27
- (D) ${}^{-}91$

7. $1.72 \times .34 =$

- (A) 584.4
- (B) 58.48
- (C) 5.848
- (D) 0.5848

8. $\frac{3}{8} \div \frac{4}{5} =$

- (F) $\frac{15}{32}$
- (G) $\frac{3}{10}$
- (H) $\frac{17}{40}$
- (J) $1\frac{5}{8}$

4. $3\frac{5}{6} + 5\frac{1}{4} =$

- (F) $8\frac{5}{6}$
- (G) 9
- (H) $9\frac{1}{12}$
- (J) $9\frac{1}{6}$

GO ON

978-1-62057-600-7 *Spectrum Test Practice 8*

MATH: COMPUTATION
SAMPLE TEST (cont.)

9. **10% of $47.00 =**
- (A) $4.70
- (B) $0.37
- (C) $0.47
- (D) none of these

10. **3807.60 − 0.23 =**
- (F) 3807.33
- (G) 3807.4
- (H) 3807.43
- (J) none of these

11. **85% of ___ = 68**
- (A) 8.0
- (B) 0.80
- (C) 60.0
- (D) none of these

12. $2\frac{1}{3} + 4\frac{1}{6} + 5\frac{1}{4} =$
- (F) 12
- (G) $11\frac{1}{2}$
- (H) $11\frac{3}{4}$
- (J) none of these

13. **82 ÷ 4 =**
- (A) 4
- (B) 64
- (C) 16
- (D) none of these

14. **⁻30 x ⁻9 =**
- (F) ⁻270
- (G) 270
- (H) ⁻39
- (J) none of these

15. $\frac{3}{4} \times \frac{1}{2} \times \frac{3}{5} =$
- (A) $\frac{7}{11}$
- (B) $1\frac{17}{20}$
- (C) $\frac{9}{40}$
- (D) none of these

16. $5\frac{1}{2} \times 3\frac{1}{6} =$
- (F) $8\frac{2}{3}$
- (G) $17\frac{5}{12}$
- (H) $15\frac{1}{12}$
- (J) $15\frac{2}{3}$

GO ON

17.
$$9.72$$
$$+\ 15.969$$

  (A) 25.689
  (B) 2.568
  (C) 25.698
  (D) 2.5698

18. $42\overline{)12.222}$

  (F) 2.910
  (G) 0.291
  (H) 0.289
  (J) 2.890

19. $\frac{11}{12} - \frac{1}{4} =$

  (A) $\frac{10}{12}$
  (B) $\frac{8}{12}$
  (C) $\frac{3}{4}$
  (D) $1\frac{1}{4}$

20. $\frac{3}{5} \times \frac{1}{10} \times \frac{1}{2} =$

  (F) $\frac{3}{100}$
  (G) $\frac{3}{10}$
  (H) $\frac{5}{100}$
  (J) $\frac{25}{10}$

21.
$$78,212$$
$$4,987$$
$$+\ 12,735$$

  (A) 92,484
  (B) 93,933
  (C) 95,234
  (D) 95,934

22. $14\overline{)28,028}$

  (F) 2,002
  (G) 20,020
  (H) 2,020
  (J) 20,200

23. **What percent of the bar is darkened?**

  (A) 30%
  (B) 50%
  (C) 70%
  (D) 90%

24. **What percent of the bar is darkened?**

  (F) 5%
  (G) 20%
  (H) 40%
  (J) 80%

STOP

Name _____ Date _____

MATH: APPLICATIONS

● Lesson 11: Geometry

Directions: Find the correct answer to each geometry problem. Fill in the circle that corresponds to your choice.

A. Look at the triangle on the right. What is the measure of the third angle?

- (A) 140°
- (B) 80°
- (C) 60°
- (D) 40°

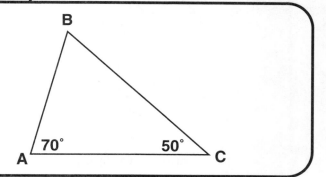

Clue Read the question carefully and think about what you are supposed to do. Look for key words, numbers, and figures before you choose an answer.

● Practice

1. The map below shows the distances between six cities in Pima County. Suppose you wanted to go from Mathtown to Circleville. What is the shortest distance you must travel?

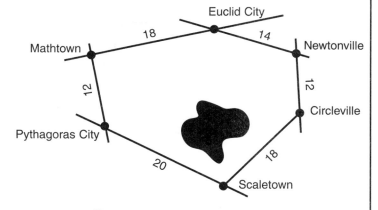

- (A) 30 miles
- (B) 50 miles
- (C) 44 miles
- (D) 64 miles

2. What is the volume of a freezer that is 5 feet high, 4 feet wide, and 3 feet deep?

- (F) 42 ft.³
- (G) 58 ft.³
- (H) 60 ft.³
- (J) 72 ft.³

3. Which number sentence shows how to find the area of a lawn that is 10 yards by 20 yards?

- (A) area = 2 x 10 yd. + 2 x 20 yd.
- (B) area = 10 yd. x 20 yd.
- (C) area = 10 ft. x 20 ft.
- (D) 86 square meters

4. Which of these is an acute angle?

- (F) 90°
- (G) 118°
- (H) 15°
- (J) 0°

GO ON

MATH: APPLICATIONS

● Lesson 11: Geometry (cont.)

5. **Which of the following best expresses the size of the solid below?**

(A) a triangular prism with dimensions of 3 cm by 3 cm by 3 cm

(B) a cube with dimensions of 3 cm by 3 cm by 3 cm

(C) a rectangular prism with dimensions of 3 cm by 6 cm by 3 cm

(D) a cube with dimensions of 3 cm by 6 cm by 3 cm

6. **What is the volume of the solid found in number 5?**

(F) 27 cm²

(G) 27 cm³

(H) 54 cm²

(J) 54 cm³

7. **Which of these statements is not true?**

(A) Two rays make up an angle.

(B) Perpendicular lines intersect.

(C) A right angle contains 90°.

(D) Parallel lines meet only at a 90° angle.

8. **Find the area of the figure below:**

20"

24"

24"

(F) 720 in.²

(G) 576 in.²

(H) 618 in.²

(J) 816 in.²

9. **What is the area of this 16-inch pizza? (A 16-inch pizza has a 16-inch diameter.)**

(A) 50.24 in.²

(B) 200.96 in.²

(C) 100.48 in.²

(D) 803.84 in.²

πr

r

10. **A 16-inch pizza costs $13.99. Find the cost per square inch to the nearest cent.**

(F) $0.02

(G) $0.06

(H) $0.07

(J) $0.14

GO ON

Name _____ Date_____

● **Lesson 11: Geometry (cont.)**

11. If point P and point Q are two vertices of a right triangle, which of these could be coordinates of the missing vertex?

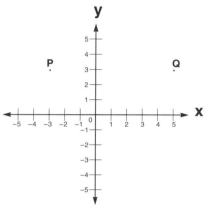

   Ⓐ (4, 1)
   Ⓑ (0, 0)
   Ⓒ (⁻4, ⁻1)
   Ⓓ (⁻3, ⁻1)

12. Which of the following lines are parallel?

Ⓕ

Ⓖ

Ⓗ

Ⓙ

13. The two figures below are similar. What is the perimeter of the larger figure?

   Ⓐ 66 in.
   Ⓑ 33 in.
   Ⓒ 28 in.
   Ⓓ 22 in.

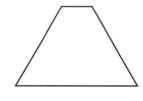

14. Find the volume of a square pyramid 6 feet high with a base 10 feet on a side.

   Ⓕ 600 ft.³
   Ⓖ 300 ft.³
   Ⓗ 200 ft.³
   Ⓙ 100 ft.³

15. Which of the following best estimates the area of Tennessee?

   Ⓐ 41,800 mi.²
   Ⓑ 20,900 mi.²
   Ⓒ 30,000 mi.²
   Ⓓ 38,412 mi.²

16. Find the area of the figure below:

   Ⓕ 900 ft.²
   Ⓖ 648 ft.²
   Ⓗ 324 ft.²
   Ⓙ 812 ft.²

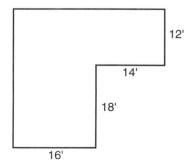

STOP

Name _____   Date_____

─────────────── **MATH: APPLICATIONS** ───────────────

Lesson 12: Congruence and Similarity

Directions: Choose the best answer for each question.

Examples

A. What translation was used to get from the shaded figure to the unshaded figure?

- (A) 6 units to the left and 4 units down
- (B) 6 units to the right and 4 units down
- (C) 6 units to the left and 4 units up
- (D) 6 units to the right and 4 units up

B. Which angle is a reflection of ∠1?

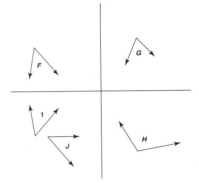

- (F) ∠F
- (G) ∠G
- (H) ∠H
- (J) ∠J

Practice

1. Three of the pairs show congruent figures. Which does not?

- (A)
- (B)
- (C)
- (D)

2. Which shows the rotation of a line segment?

- (F)
- (G)
- (H)
- (J)

GO ON

978-1-62057-600-7 *Spectrum Test Practice 8*

Name _____   Date_____

MATH: APPLICATIONS

● **Lesson 12: Congruence and Similarity (cont.)**

3. **Which is a correct explanation for how to find the measure of ∠7?**

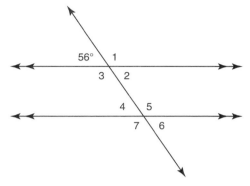

(A) Two angles, ∠4 and the 56° angle, are corresponding angles, so the measure of ∠4 is 56°. Two angles, ∠4 and ∠7, are supplementary because they are a linear pair, so the measure of ∠7 is 124°.

(B) Two angles, ∠1 and the 56° angle, are supplementary, so the measure of ∠1 is 124°. Two angles, ∠1 and ∠7, are congruent because they are alternate interior angles, so the measure of ∠7 is also 124°.

(C) Two angles, ∠3 and the 56° angle, are supplementary, so the measure of ∠3 is 124°. Two angles, ∠3 and ∠7, are congruent because they are alternate interior angles, so the measure of ∠5 is also 56°.

(D) Two angles, ∠2 and the 56° angle, are vertical angles, so the measure of ∠2 is 56°. Two angles, ∠2 and ∠7, are congruent because they are corresponding angles, so the measure of ∠7 is also 56°.

4. **Which pair of transformations can be used on Figure A to get Figure B?**

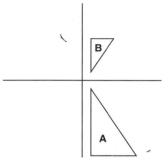

(F) translation up, then a dilation with a scale factor of $\frac{1}{2}$

(G) translation down, then a dilation with a scale factor of 2

(H) vertical reflection, then a dilation with a scale factor of $\frac{1}{2}$

(J) vertical reflection, then a dilation with a scale factor of 2

5. **Which set of points gives a reflection of the figure shown over the *y*–axis?**

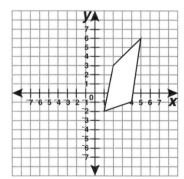

(A) (2, ⁻3), (1, 2), (4, 1), and (5, ⁻6)

(B) (⁻2, 3), (⁻1, ⁻2), (⁻4, ⁻1), and (⁻5, 6)

(C) (⁻2, ⁻3), (⁻1, 2), (⁻4, 1), and (⁻5, ⁻6)

(D) (2, 3), (1, ⁻2), (4, ⁻1), and (5, 6)

STOP

Name _____   Date _____

MATH: APPLICATIONS

● **Lesson 13: The Pythagorean Theorem**

Directions: Choose the best answer for each question.

Examples

A. **What is the length of the missing side?**

- (A) 17 centimeters
- (B) 12 centimeters
- (C) 9 centimeters
- (D) 6 centimeters

15 cm

9 cm

B. **What is the shortest distance between points *A* and *B*?**

- (F) 13
- (G) $\sqrt{85}$
- (H) $\sqrt{89}$
- (J) 13

● **Practice**

1. **Which of these could be a right triangle?**

- (A) 9, 13, 9
- (B) 10, 16, 14
- (C) 11, 19, 17
- (D) 15, 36, 39

2. **Which set of measures does not make a right triangle?**

- (F) 3, 4, 5
- (G) 8, 15, 17
- (H) 5, 11, 12
- (J) 7, 24, 25

3. **What is the greatest linear distance between any two points on a cube with sides that measure 10 meters?**

- (A) 10 meters
- (B) $10\sqrt{2}$ meters
- (C) $10\sqrt{3}$ meters
- (D) 20 meters

4. **What is the distance between points *A* and *B*?**

- (F) $6\sqrt{2}$
- (G) $\sqrt{74}$
- (H) 9
- (J) 12

5. **Television screens are sold by the measure of the diagonal of the screen. A 30-inch television screen measures 24 inches from left to right. How tall is the screen of this television?**

- (A) 6 inches
- (B) 12 inches
- (C) 18 inches
- (D) 24 inches

978-1-62057-600-7 *Spectrum Test Practice 8*

Name _____   Date_____

MATH: APPLICATIONS

● Lesson 14: Measurement

Directions: Find the correct answer to each measurement problem. Fill in the circle that corresponds to your choice.

Example

A. How many centimeters long is WY?

- Ⓐ 4 centimeters
- Ⓑ 5 centimeters
- Ⓒ 6 centimeters
- Ⓓ 3 centimeters

Clue If you are confused by a problem, read it again. If you are still confused, skip the problem and come back to it later. For some problems, you will have to work on scratch paper. Be sure to transfer numbers accurately and compute carefully.

● Practice

1. Suppose you had 5 coins in your pocket totaling $0.53. Which of the following statements is true about the coins?
   - Ⓐ Some of the coins are nickels.
   - Ⓑ Two of the coins are dimes.
   - Ⓒ Two of the coins are quarters.
   - Ⓓ None of the coins are pennies.

2. Which of the following comes closest to the diameter of a dinner plate?
   - Ⓕ 30 mm
   - Ⓖ 30 cm
   - Ⓗ 30 dm
   - Ⓙ 30 m

3. Which of these is the greatest volume?
   - Ⓐ 36 pints
   - Ⓑ 24 quarts
   - Ⓒ 4 gallons
   - Ⓓ 60 cups

4. If you convert pounds to kilograms by dividing by 2.2, how many kg are there in a 10-pound bag of charcoal?
   - Ⓕ 10 kg
   - Ⓖ 8.6 kg
   - Ⓗ 4.54 kg
   - Ⓙ 3.63 kg

5. Which of the following comes closest to the estimate of the number of grams in two objects weighing 1,945 mg and 1,382 mg?
   - Ⓐ 1 g
   - Ⓑ 2 g
   - Ⓒ 3 g
   - Ⓓ 4 g

GO ON

MATH: APPLICATIONS

● Lesson 14: Measurement (cont.)

6. A bus was scheduled to leave the station at 3:15 P.M. Because of a rainstorm, the bus was delayed for 3 hours and 50 minutes. What time did the bus leave the station?

   F) 6:30 P.M.
   G) 6:50 P.M.
   H) 7:05 P.M.
   J) 7:15 P.M.

7. A worker had a roll of tape that was 10 yards long. She cut 7 feet of tape from the roll. How much tape was left on the roll?

   A) 8 yards
   B) 7 yards and 2 feet
   C) 6 yards and 2 feet
   D) 9 yards

8. How many inches are in 13 feet?

   F) 144
   G) 86
   H) 156
   J) 13

9. Which comes closest to the length of an unsharpened pencil?

   A) 6 inches
   B) 6 centimeters
   C) 6 millimeters
   D) 6 feet

10. Which of these would be purchased by the ton?

    F) gasoline
    G) gravel
    H) potatoes
    J) milk

11. Which of these rooms probably measures 12 feet by 11 feet?

    A) bathroom
    B) bedroom
    C) pantry
    D) hall closet

12. Which works best in measuring the height of a mountain?

    F) yards
    G) inches
    H) feet
    J) centimeters

13. What fraction of a yard is 27 inches?

    A) $\frac{1}{2}$
    B) $\frac{2}{3}$
    C) $\frac{3}{4}$
    D) $\frac{5}{6}$

14. Which comes closest to the length of a loaf of garlic bread?

    F) 1 meter
    G) 5 decimeters
    H) 180 millimeters
    J) 18 centimeters

15. 862 millimeters is equal to—

    A) 0.862 meters
    B) 8.620 meters
    C) 86.2 meters
    D) 0.0862 meters

STOP

Name _____ Date _____

MATH: APPLICATIONS

● Lesson 15: Volume

Directions: Choose the best answer for each question.

Examples

A. What is the volume of a sphere with a radius of 9 cm?

- (A) 324π cm³
- (B) 486π cm³
- (C) 972π cm³
- (D) 808π cm³

B. What is the volume of a cone with a height of 10mm and a radius of 6mm?

- (F) 120π mm³
- (G) 96π mm³
- (H) 108π mm³
- (J) 60π mm³

● Practice

1. What is the volume?

- (A) 216π cubic units
- (B) 972π cubic units
- (C) 378π cubic units
- (D) 108π cubic units

2. What is the volume?

- (F) $5,461\frac{1}{3}$ π m³
- (G) $682\frac{2}{3}$ π m³
- (H) 1,024π m³
- (J) 256π m³

3. A basketball has a volume of 4500π cubic centimeters. What is its radius?

- (A) 10 cm
- (B) 30 cm
- (C) 15 cm
- (D) 25 cm

4. The cylinder has a volume of 2,500π cm³. What is its height?

- (F) 1 cm
- (G) 2 cm
- (H) 4 cm
- (J) 8 cm

5. An ice cream cone has a spherical scoop on it with the same radius as the cone. If the ice cream melts into the cone, it will fill the cone exactly. Which statement is true?

- (A) The height of the cone is 4 times its radius.
- (B) The height of the cone is 2 times its radius.
- (C) The height of the cone is $\frac{1}{2}$ its radius.
- (D) The height of the cone is $\frac{1}{4}$ its radius.

STOP

MATH: APPLICATIONS

● **Lesson 16: Problem Solving**

Directions: Find the correct answer to each problem. Fill in the space that corresponds to your choice.

Examples

A. A lake is normally 42 feet deep. Which number sentence shows the depth after a storm makes the lake 3 feet deeper?

- (A) 42 − 3 = ☐
- (B) 42 + 3 = ☐
- (C) 42 x 3 = ☐
- (D) 42 ÷ 3 = ☐

B. Samuel bought 80 small baskets of tomatoes at $1.50 each and sold them for $4.00 each. How much did she make altogether?

- (F) $150
- (G) $200
- (H) $275
- (J) Not given

 Clue Read each problem carefully. Look for key words, numbers, and figures on each problem. If you must work on scratch paper, be sure you perform the correct operation.

● **Practice**

1. Ten square tables, each seating one person per side, are pushed together to form one long rectangular table. How many people can be seated?

- (A) 20
- (B) 22
- (C) 24
- (D) 28

2. Terry has 6 blue shirts, 5 green shirts, and 3 striped shirts. If 2 of the blue shirts are also striped, how many shirts are there?

- (F) 14
- (G) 12
- (H) 10
- (J) 4

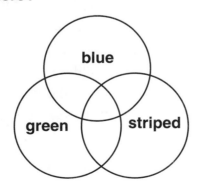

3. If the truck used 25 gallons of gas to travel 375 miles, how far can it go with 4 gallons?

- (A) 96 miles
- (B) 50 miles
- (C) 56 miles
- (D) 60 miles

4. Jason is 6 feet tall and casts a shadow of 5 feet. If he stands next to a tree that casts a 10-foot shadow, how tall is the tree?

- (F) 10 feet
- (G) 12 feet
- (H) 14 feet
- (J) 8 feet

6'

5'

10'

GO ON

Name _____ Date _____

● **Lesson 16: Problem Solving (cont.)**

On string instruments, placing your finger at different places along the string produces different sound intervals. For example, placing your finger $\frac{3}{4}$ of the string length from the bridge will produce a fourth interval. The chart below is used for numbers 5 and 6, and shows the needed ratio of string length from the bridge to produce the given interval.

INTERVAL	RATIO
third	$\frac{4}{5}$
fourth	$\frac{3}{4}$
fifth	$\frac{2}{3}$
sixth	$\frac{3}{5}$
octave	$\frac{1}{2}$

5. A cello string is 24 in. from the bridge to the scroll. How far from the bridge would you place your finger to produce a fifth interval?

     (A) 20 in.
     (B) 10 in.
     (C) 16 in.
     (D) 14 in.

6. For an instrument with a 10-inch string, where would you place your finger to play a third interval?

     (F) 6 in.
     (G) 8 in.
     (H) 10 in.
     (J) not given

7. Travis and Marty had $45 to spend on gifts for their parents. They both had earned the money, but Travis had earned $5 more than Marty. How much did Marty earn?

     (A) $20
     (B) $25
     (C) $15
     (D) $30

8. Phyllis bought sneakers for $59. The next week, the sneakers went on sale for 25% off. How much would Phyllis have saved if she had waited for the sale?

     (F) $20.00
     (G) $14.25
     (H) $14.75
     (J) $11.50

9. A softball player gets a hit 4 times out of every 11 times she comes to bat. She batted 44 times last season. How many hits did she get?

     (A) 11
     (B) 44
     (C) 4
     (D) 16

10. Which data does not belong?

     (F) 1 hr.
     (G) 60 min.
     (H) 12 in.
     (J) 3600 sec.

1 hr.	60 min.
12 in.	3600 sec.

11. Which data does not belong?

     (A) 123
     (B) 555
     (C) 321
     (D) 231

123	231
555	321

GO ON

——— MATH: APPLICATIONS ———

● **Lesson 16: Problem Solving (cont.)**

12. **A grill holds two steaks. What is the shortest time to grill 3 steaks if each side takes 10 minutes to cook?**
    - (F) 10 minutes
    - (G) 20 minutes
    - (H) 25 minutes
    - (J) 30 minutes

13. **The number of water lilies in a pond doubles each day. From the time one lily was placed in a pond until the time the pond was completely covered with lilies took 30 days. After how many days was the pond half covered?**
    - (A) 15 days
    - (B) 16 days
    - (C) 29 days
    - (D) not enough information

14. **Two truckers drove from Dayton to Toledo and back. The first trucker drove to Toledo at 50 mph and returned to Dayton at 60 mph. The second trucker drove to Toledo and back at 57 mph. If the round trip is 300 miles, which driver took longer to make the round trip?**
    - (F) first trucker
    - (G) second trucker
    - (H) they both had same amount of time
    - (J) not enough information

15. **Which of these sampling methods will give the best random sample of 65 students from the entire school population of 650?**
    - (A) Choose the 65 students in Mr. Green's advanced computer classes.
    - (B) Select the first 65 students that walk out the front door of school at the end of the day.
    - (C) Choose the 65 students with the highest grade point average.
    - (D) Select the 65 oldest children at the school.

16. **The table shows the number of students who went to the snack bar after school on the first four days that it was open. If the pattern continues, how many students will go to the snack bar after school on day 5?**

Day	Number of Students
1	78
2	89
3	101
4	114
5	

- (F) 125
- (G) 126
- (H) 127
- (J) 128

STOP

Name _____ Date_____

━━━━━━━━━━━━━━━━━━ **MATH: APPLICATIONS** ━━━━━━━━━━━━━━━━━━

● **Lesson 17: Algebra**

Directions: Find the correct answer to each measurement problem. Mark the space for your choice.

Examples

A. What is the value of y in the number sentence $4y + 3 = 19$?

(A) 9
(B) 2
(C) 3
(D) 4

B. 36 more than x is 94. Which equation shows this problem?

(F) $x + 36 = 94$
(G) $x - 36 = 94$
(H) $94 \div 36 = x$
(J) $36 - x = 94$

Clue If you are sure you know which answer is correct, mark the space for your answer and move to the next problem. Before you choose an answer, ask yourself, "Does this answer make sense?"

● **Practice**

1. What is the missing weight in the balance below?

(A) 2
(B) 4
(C) 6
(D) 8

2. What weight should n be to balance this level?

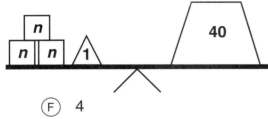

(F) 4
(G) 17
(H) 5
(J) 13

3. Which square has the wrong fraction?

$\frac{2}{3}$	X	$\frac{5}{8}$	=	A $\frac{5}{12}$
X		X		X
B $\frac{3}{4}$	X	C $\frac{4}{5}$	=	$\frac{3}{5}$
=		=		=
$\frac{1}{2}$	X	D $\frac{1}{4}$	=	$\frac{1}{4}$

(A) $\frac{5}{12}$
(B) $\frac{3}{4}$
(C) $\frac{4}{5}$
(D) $\frac{1}{4}$

4. What is the value of x in this equation?

$\frac{3}{8} \times \frac{8}{x} = 1$

(F) 2
(G) 3
(H) 6
(J) 4

GO ON

978-1-62057-600-7 *Spectrum Test Practice 8*

MATH: APPLICATIONS

● Lesson 17: Algebra (cont.)

5. For which of these equations would *a* = 8 when *b* = 12?

   (A) $2a - b = 14$

   (B) $2b - a = 22$

   (●) $2a + b = 28$

   (D) $b - a = 10$

6. What label goes in the blank on the Venn diagram below?

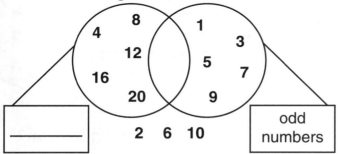

   odd numbers

   2 6 10

   (F) Prime numbers

   (●) Multiples of 4

   (H) Even numbers less than 30

   (J) Mid-sized numbers

7. Bob owns a small construction company. His job is to estimate the cost to build houses. One of the equations he uses is $C = A \times \$89.00$, where *A* is the area in square feet of the house and $89.00 is the average cost of construction per square foot. What do you think the *C* stands for?

   (A) The number of square feet in the house

   (B) The cost of finishing each room in the house

   (C) The real estate broker's commission

   (●) The building cost to the owner

8. If $6 < a$ and $a < b$, what symbol should replace the blank in the expression *b* _____ 5?

   (F) <

   (G) =

   (H) >

   (J) –

9. What number must be subtracted from 10 to get a number that is less than ⁻3?

   (A) a number greater than 13

   (B) a number less than 10

   (C) a number greater than 4

   (D) a number between ⁻3 and 10

10. If *a* = 6 and *b* = 12, what is the value of the expression $\frac{(4a + b)}{6} =$

   (F) 5

   (G) 6

   (H) 10

   (J) ⁻2

11. Suppose that *a* and *b* are positive numbers and that $a > b$. What is always true about the ratio $(a \times 2) \div (b \times 2)$?

   (A) The ratio is less than one.

   (B) The ratio is more than one.

   (C) The ratio is equal to one.

   (D) The ratio is a negative number.

12. If $3y + 0 = 36$ then $y =$

   (F) 24

   (G) 8

   (H) 12

   (J) 14

STOP

MATH: APPLICATIONS

● Lesson 18: Linear Equations

Directions: Choose the best answer for each question.

Examples

A. The sum of two numbers is 24. The difference of the two numbers is 6. What is the larger of the two numbers?

- (A) 9
- (B) 12
- (C) 15
- (D) 18

B. What ordered pair is true for both $3x + y = 7$ and $2y + 6x = 12$?

- (F) (1, 3)
- (G) (2, 1)
- (H) There is no solution.
- (J) The two equations represent the same line.

● Practice

1. Which ordered pair is true for both $2x - 3y = 12$ and $2x + y = 4$?

- (A) (⁻3, 8)
- (B) (1, 2)
- (C) (3, ⁻2)
- (D) (⁻3, 2)

2. Use the graph to find the solution of $y = ⁻x - 2$ and $y = \frac{x}{2} + 4$.

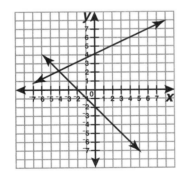

- (F) (⁻2, 0)
- (G) (0, ⁻2)
- (H) (⁻4, ⁻6)
- (J) (⁻4, 2)

3. Eric has $80 on Day 1 and spends $8 each day. Susan has $60 on Day 1 and spends $4 each day. When will they have the same amount of money?

- (A) on the third day
- (B) on the fourth day
- (C) on the fifth day
- (D) on the sixth day

4. What is the solution to the system of equations?

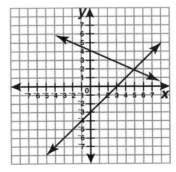

- (F) (3, 0)
- (G) (0, 4)
- (H) (2, 5)
- (J) (5, 2)

STOP

MATH: APPLICATIONS

● **Lesson 19: Functions**

Directions: Choose the best answer for each question.

> ### Example
>
> **A. Compare the functions described. Which has the greater rate of change?**
>
> **Function 1 includes the points (1, 3), (4, 7), (10, 15), and (19, 27).**
>
> **Function 2 is defined by the equation** $y = \frac{3x}{4} + 5$.
>
> (A) Function 1 has the greater rate of change.
>
> (B) Function 2 has the greater rate of change.
>
> (C) Both functions have the same rate of change.
>
> (D) The rate of change varies within each function.

● **Practice**

1. **Three of the tables show functions. Which one is not a function?**

(A)
Input	1	4	7	11
Output	11	7	4	1

(B)
Input	5	6	7	8
Output	10	0	12	0

(C)
Input	0	2	4	4
Output	3	6	8	9

(D)
Input	0	2	4	6
Output	3	3	3	3

2. **A math teacher determines how much time to allow for a quiz using the formula described below. What might the numbers 0.75 and 5 mean in the context of this problem?**

$T = 0.75n + 5$, where T is the time in minutes and n is the number of problems on the quiz.

(F) The quiz should take a minimum of 0.75 minutes plus 5 minutes per problem.

(G) The quiz should take a minimum of 5 minutes plus 0.75 minutes per problem.

(H) Each problem on the quiz should take 5.75 minutes.

(J) The entire quiz should take 5.75 minutes.

3. **Which is the graph of a function?**

(A)

(B)

(C)

(D)

 GO ON

MATH: APPLICATIONS

● Lesson 19: Functions (cont.)

4. Darlene begins a book that is 489 pages long. She reads 30 pages in an hour. Let h represent the number of hours that Darlene has spent reading the book and p represent the number of pages she has left to read. Which function describes the number of pages she has left to read?

  Ⓕ $p = 489 - 30h$

  Ⓖ $p = 30h - 489$

  Ⓗ $p = \frac{489}{h}$ (23)

  Ⓙ $p = h(489 - 30)$

5. Three of the equations describe linear functions. Which one does not?

  Ⓐ $y = \frac{4}{x} + 5$

  Ⓑ $y = 4x + 5$

  Ⓒ $y = \frac{x}{4} + 5$

  Ⓓ $y = \frac{4}{5}$

6. Think about how the graph of each situation would look. Choose the best description.
  Situation 1: Miguel has $30 at the beginning of the week. Each day, he spends $5.
  Situation 2: Adrianna has $30 at the beginning of the week. Each day, she earns $5.

  Ⓕ Miguel's graph would begin at (0, 30) and have a negative slope. Adrianna's graph would begin at (0, 0) and have a positive slope.

  Ⓖ Miguel's graph would begin at (0, ⁻30). Adrianna's graph would begin at (0, 30). The slopes of both graphs would be the same.

  Ⓗ Both graphs would begin at (0, 30). The slope of Miguel's graph would be negative, but the slope of Adrianna's graph would be positive.

  Ⓙ Both graphs would begin at (0, 30). The slopes would be the same.

7. Which equation describes a linear function?

  Ⓐ $3\sqrt{x}$

  Ⓑ $3x^2 + 4x + 5 = 9y$

  Ⓒ $3xy = 9$

  Ⓓ $3x + 4y = 9$

8. T-shirts cost $15 for the first shirt and $12 for each additional shirt. Which graph shows this situation?

  Ⓕ

  Ⓖ

  Ⓗ

  Ⓙ

GO ON

● **Lesson 19: Functions (cont.)**

9. Sarah plans an 18-km bike ride to a nearby pond. She rides her bicycle at a rate of 12 km per hour. The equation $d = 12t$ describes the distance she bicycles toward the pond. What values of t make sense for this problem?

   (A) all positive numbers

   (B) $0 \le t \le 1.5$

   (C) $0 \le t \le 18$

   (D) $t \ge 1.5$

10. Which equation could be used to complete this function table?

X	y
⁻2	⁻9
0	⁻3
3	6
6	
9	
15	

   (F) $y = \dfrac{x}{3} - 3$

   (G) $y = x - 7$

   (H) $y = 2x - 5$

   (J) $y = 3x - 3$

11. Nicole walks from her house to her friend's house. She waits there for a few minutes, then she gets in a car with her friend's family. Together, they ride on the highway to their destination. Which graph shows the distance Nicole travels?

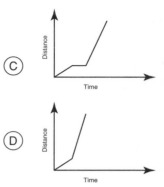

12. Compare the costs of three brands of socks. Order them from least expensive to most expensive.

   Brand A:

Pairs of Socks	2	6	8
Total Cost	$5.50	$16.50	$22.00

   Brand B:

   Brand C: $C = 2.5s$, where s is the pairs of socks, and C is the total cost

   (F) Brand A, Brand B, Brand C

   (G) Brand C, Brand A, Brand B

   (H) Brand B, Brand A, Brand C

   (J) Brand C, Brand B, Brand A

13. Which set of coordinates describes a function?

   (A) (0, 3), (2, ⁻4), (⁻7, 8), (12, 8), (9, ⁻6)

   (B) (0, ⁻3), (2, 4), (⁻7, 9), (2, 8), (9, 6)

   (C) (⁻8, 3), (⁻4, 4), (0, 8), (0, 12), (4, 6)

   (D) (⁻3, 3), (⁻2, 4), (⁻1, 5), (0, 6), (⁻2, 6)

STOP

Name _____   Date _____

MATH: APPLICATIONS

● Lesson 20: Patterns in Data

Directions: Use the information about Lana's business to answer numbers 1–4.

Lana makes and sells paintings. The amount she sells each painting for (*y*) is based on the time in hours that she spends on each painting (*x*). The equation $y = 50x + 10$ provides an approximation for the cost of each painting.

1. **What might 50 mean in $y = 50x + 10$?**
   - (A) a $50 minimum charge
   - (B) $50 per painting sold
   - (C) $50 per hour spent painting
   - (D) 50 times what Lana spends on the materials

2. **What might 10 mean in $y = 50x + 10$?**
   - (F) $10 for canvas and paint
   - (G) a $10 discount on the price
   - (H) $10 per hour spent painting
   - (J) 10 hours

3. **If it takes 6 more hours for Lana to finish a painting, about how much more will the painting cost?**
   - (A) $6
   - (B) $30
   - (C) $150
   - (D) $300

4. **Which scatterplot and line of best fit could illustrate Lana's art business?**

(F)

(G)

(H)

(J)

GO ON

978-1-62057-600-7 *Spectrum Test Practice 8*

═══ MATH: APPLICATIONS ═══

● **Lesson 20: Patterns in Data (cont.)**

Directions: Use the scatterplot to answer numbers 5–7. Use the data about biking to answer numbers 8–10.

5. Mr. Chepke made the scatterplot to compare his students' final grades with the number of homework assignments they did not turn in. What type of association does the plot show?

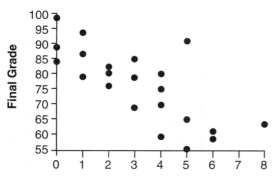

Missed Homework Assignments

- (A) linear positive association
- (B) linear negative association
- (C) nonlinear association
- (D) no association

6. Which equation could describe a line of best fit for the data?

- (F) $y = 85$
- (G) $y = {}^-5x + 100$
- (H) $y = {}^-5x + 90$
- (J) $y = 5x + 65$

7. Which point is an outlier?

- (A) (0, 97)
- (B) (5, 92)
- (C) (8, 64)
- (D) There are no outliers.

8. The table shows the results of a survey. What percentage of students who live within 1 kilometer of a bicycle path ride a bicycle at least once a week?

Do You Ride a Bicycle at Least Once a Week?

Where Do You Live?	Yes	No
Within 1 kilometer of bicycle path	30	10
More than 1 kilometer from bicycle path	15	45

- (F) 30%
- (G) 80%
- (H) 75%
- (J) $66\frac{2}{3}$%

9. What percentage of students who ride a bicycle at least once a week live within 1 kilometer of a bicycle path?

- (A) 70%
- (B) 30%
- (C) $66\frac{2}{3}$%
- (D) 50%

10. What can you conclude?

- (F) There is no correlation between where students live and how often they ride bicycles.
- (G) Bicycles are not allowed except on bicycle paths.
- (H) Students who ride bicycles frequently are more likely to live farther from bicycle paths.
- (J) Students who ride bicycles frequently are more likely to live near bicycle paths.

STOP

Name _____ Date_____

MATH: APPLICATIONS
SAMPLE TEST

Directions: Read and work each problem. Fill in the circle that corresponds to your choice.

Examples

A. Kate bought 6 packs of gum. Each pack has 24 pieces. If Kate chews an average of 12 pieces each week, how long will the gum last?

- (A) 6 weeks
- (B) 3 months
- (C) 6 years
- (D) 6 days

B. What is the area of a warehouse that is 150 feet by 300 feet?

- (F) 40,000 ft.²
- (G) 45,000 ft.²
- (H) 90,000 ft.²
- (J) 100,000 ft.²

---

1. Tyler has a great part-time job that requires him to work three 4-hour shifts through the week, and one 8-hour shift on the weekend. How many hours does he work each week?

- (A) 8 hours
- (B) 12 hours
- (C) 20 hours
- (D) 49 hours

2. Stephanie had a submarine sandwich and a soft drink for $5.28. Alyson ordered the same thing. Jeanie and Angie split a pizza that cost $13.00 and each had a soft drink that cost $1.25. Which of the following would be the closest to a 20% tip on the total purchase?

- (F) $2.00
- (G) $2.50
- (H) $4.00
- (J) $5.00

3. The Riverwalk Mall has increased its number of stores by 30% in the past 3 years. Three years ago there were 160 stores. How many are there now?

- (A) 160
- (B) 180
- (C) 48
- (D) 208

4. Which of these angles is less than 90°?

- (F) ∠ abc
- (G) ∠ efg
- (H) ∠ hij
- (J) ∠ klm

5. Subtract to find the area of the shaded area.

- (A) 49 in.²
- (B) 24.5 in.²
- (C) 10.5 in.²
- (D) 18.5 in.²

7"

7"

GO ON

---

6. Ron was given a bag of colored candy pieces and asked to figure some odds. He counted 42 red pieces, 25 yellow pieces, 10 green pieces, and 13 blue pieces. He put all the candy pieces into a jar, stirred them up, and then poured one out of the jar. What were the odds that it was a green one?

     (F) 1 in 4
     (G) 1 in 9
     (H) 1 in 10
     (J) 2 in 5

7. A roll of tape contained 2 meters. If each box required 50 centimeters of tape, how many boxes could be secured with one roll of tape?

     (A) 2
     (B) 4
     (C) 6
     (D) 8

8. Below is a diagram of an expression used by a framing company for determining the number of 1 in. by 1 in. tiles needed to frame a square trivet. The size of the square trivet below is 4 inches on each side. How many tiles are needed to frame it?

     (F) 16
     (G) 20
     (H) 18
     (J) 22

9. A taxi driver works five days a week. This week he drove 268 miles, 242 miles, 310 miles, and 224 miles. What is the average distance he drove this week?

     (A) 228 miles
     (B) 216 miles
     (C) 261 miles
     (D) 284 miles

10. Pamela has a truck that is 1.1 meters long, 0.4 meters high, and 0.7 meters wide. What is the volume of the truck?

     (F) 0.308 m³
     (G) 2.2 m³
     (H) 30.8 m³
     (J) 4.4 m³

11. Two integers have a product of 100, and their sum, when divided in half, equals 26. What are the integers?

     (A) 10 and 10
     (B) 2 and 50
     (C) 5 and 20
     (D) not enough information

12. For which of these equations would $x = 6$ when $y = 12$?

     (F) $x = 3y$
     (G) $x = 2y$
     (H) $x = \frac{1}{2}y$
     (J) $x = \frac{1}{3}y$

GO ON

Name _____   Date_____

13. Which of these is the greatest volume?

    (A) 4500 milliliters

    (B) 450 liters

    (C) 450 milliliters

    (D) 45 kiloliters

14. Jamela arrived at the museum at 2:30. Michael arrived 1 hour and 10 minutes later. Alana arrived 25 minutes after Michael. At what time did Alana arrive?

    (F) 2:55

    (G) 3:40

    (H) 4:05

    (J) none of the above

15. A triangle measured 0.75 meters high and 0.4 meters wide at its base. What is the area of the triangle?

    (A) 3 m²

    (B) 0.3 m²

    (C) 1.5 m²

    (D) 0.15 m²

16. What is the circumference of the circle?

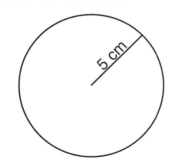

    (F) 31.4 cm

    (G) 15.7 cm

    (H) 86.3 cm

    (J) none of the above

17. What is the square root of 289?

    (A) 11

    (B) 13

    (C) 17

    (D) 19

18. There are different time zones in the United States. When it is 9:00 P.M. in New York, it is 6:00 P.M. in California. If a plane leaves New York at 8:00 A.M. New York time and lands in California at 11:00 A.M. California time, how long was the flight?

    (F) 2 hours

    (G) 6 hours

    (H) 7 hours

    (J) 8 hours

19. In triangle ABC, angle A measures 45 degrees. Angle B measured 7 degrees more than angle C. What is the measure of angle C?

    (A) 45 degrees

    (B) 71 degrees

    (C) 64 degrees

    (D) not enough information

20. For which of these equations would $a = 5$ when $b = 6$?

    (F) $a - b = 11$

    (G) $a + b = 11$

    (H) $a + b = 1$

    (J) $a - b = 1$

GO ON ➡

21. A sporting goods store is having a sale on T-shirts. If you buy one T-shirt at regular price, you can buy the second T-shirt at half price. If the regular price of one T-shirt is $11.00, how much would it cost to buy two?

    (A) $11.00
    (B) $22.00
    (C) $16.50
    (D) not enough information

22. Five people attend a dinner party. If every person shakes hands with all the other people at the party, how many handshakes will there be?

    (F) 8
    (G) 12
    (H) 6
    (J) 10

23. Jackie entered the elevator on the floor where her mom is located. She went up 3 floors, down 3 floors, and up 10 floors. She got off the elevator to attend a meeting. After the meeting, she rode the elevator down 9 floors, up 4 floors, and finally down 6 floors to the first floor to eat in the restaurant. On what floor is Jackie's mom?

    (A) 4th floor
    (B) 2nd floor
    (C) 5th floor
    (D) 9th floor

24. What is the area of the shaded portion of the figure below?

    (F) 55 units
    (G) 144 units
    (H) 89 units
    (J) 40 units

25. In the circle below, the shaded portion represents the percentage of students who passed a fitness test. What percentage of students passed the test?

    (A) 20%
    (B) 40%
    (C) 80%
    (D) 75%

Percent who passed

26. A Jaguar XJ220 traveled 217 miles/hour. How many feet/minute was the Jaguar traveling?

    (F) 10,400 ft./min.
    (G) 19,096 ft./min.
    (H) 16,084 ft./min.
    (J) 17,076 ft./min.

STOP

MATH: PRACTICE TEST

● Part 1: Concepts

Directions: Read and work each problem. Fill in the circle that corresponds to your choice.

Examples

A. Which of these decimals is equal to $\frac{3}{8}$?

- (A) 0.375
- (B) 0.78
- (C) 0.37
- (D) 0.0375

B. Of these choices, which is the smallest number that can be divided evenly by 6 and 36?

- (F) 108
- (G) 6
- (H) 54
- (J) 72

1. $\sqrt{169}$

- (A) 12
- (B) 11
- (C) 13
- (D) 14

2. The distance from Nogales to Tucson is 92 miles. From Tucson to Phoenix is 110 miles. Which numbers would you use to estimate the distance from Nogales to Phoenix by going through Tucson?

- (F) 90 and 110
- (G) 100 and 100
- (H) 120 and 110
- (J) 80 and 100

3. What is the prime factorization of 72?

- (A) 2 x 2 x 2 x 3 x 3
- (B) 6 x 6 x 2
- (C) 2 x 3 x 2 x 6
- (D) 36 x 2

4. What should replace the blank space in the number sentence below?

$$0.0043 \times \underline{\hspace{2cm}} = 43$$

- (F) 10^{-4}
- (G) 10^3
- (H) 10^4
- (J) 10^5

5. Which number sentence is true?

- (A) 2 < 0
- (B) ⁻4 > 2
- (C) 3 > ⁻1
- (D) ⁻3 < ⁻13

6. How much would the value of 364,921 increase by replacing the 3 with a 5?

- (F) 200,000
- (G) 2,000
- (H) 20,000
- (J) 200

7. Which arrow points most closely to $-\frac{3}{8}$?

- (A) M
- (B) N
- (C) O
- (D) P

GO ON

8. $\frac{5}{9} = \frac{20}{x}$

    $x =$ _____

    (F) 9
    (G) 36
    (H) 24
    (J) 15

9. Which of these is 8,425,376 rounded to the nearest hundred thousand?

    (A) 8,430,000
    (B) 8,425,000
    (C) 8,400,000
    (D) 8,425,400

10. $9^4 =$ _____

    (F) 9 x 4
    (G) 9 x 9
    (H) 9 x 9 x 9
    (J) 9 x 9 x 9 x 9

11. What number completes the number sentence below?

    13 x □ = 26 x 20

    (A) 18
    (B) 40
    (C) 26
    (D) 5

12. Which is the best estimate

    of $21\frac{1}{5}$ x 9.84?

    (F) 21 x 7
    (G) 21 x 10
    (H) 20 x 10
    (J) 20 x 5

13. What is the reciprocal of $\frac{2}{9}$?

    (A) $\frac{9}{2}$
    (B) 9 x 2
    (C) 2 x 9
    (D) 1

14. $15.18 \times 10^4 =$ _____

    (F) 0.1518
    (G) 1.5118
    (H) 1578
    (J) 151,800

15. Which of these is greater than the others?

    (A) one fourth
    (B) one and one eighth
    (C) one and three tenths
    (D) one and four hundredths

16. What is the value of the expression $(12 - 3)^2 \div 9$?

    (F) 81
    (G) 27
    (H) 18
    (J) 9

17. How would you write 37% as a fraction?

    (A) 0.37
    (B) $\frac{37}{100}$
    (C) $\frac{3}{7}$
    (D) $\frac{7}{3}$

STOP

Name _____ Date_____

● **Part 2: Computation**

Directions: Find the correct answer for each problem. Mark the space for your choice. Choose "none of these" if the correct answer is not given.

Examples

A. $^-4 \times ^-9 =$
- (A) 13
- (B) 18
- (C) 36
- (D) $^-13$

B. $\frac{1}{3} \div 3 =$
- (F) $\frac{1}{9}$
- (G) 9
- (H) $\frac{1}{6}$
- (J) 6

1. $^-50 \times ^-6 =$
- (A) $^-300$
- (B) 300
- (C) $^-56$
- (D) 56

2. $9\frac{5}{6}$
    $-\ \frac{7}{12}$
- (F) $9\frac{1}{4}$
- (G) $8\frac{1}{4}$
- (H) $9\frac{1}{3}$
- (J) $9\frac{1}{2}$

3. $0.042 \div 62 =$
- (A) 0.7
- (B) 0.007
- (C) 0.0007
- (D) 0.07

4. 30% of □ = 24
- (F) 21
- (G) 72
- (H) 80
- (J) 720

5. $\frac{3}{8} \times \frac{2}{3} =$
- (A) $\frac{4}{8}$
- (B) $\frac{1}{4}$
- (C) $\frac{6}{20}$
- (D) $\frac{1}{8}$

6. 494
    $-\ 37$
- (F) 531
- (G) 412
- (H) 487
- (J) 457

7. $0.7\overline{)567}$
- (A) 77
- (B) 870
- (C) 810
- (D) 880

8. 0.816
    $\times\ 0.456$
- (F) 0.472034
- (G) 0.370094
- (H) 0.372096
- (J) 0.352375

9. $\frac{13}{16}$
    $-\ \frac{9}{16}$
- (A) $\frac{1}{2}$
- (B) $\frac{1}{4}$
- (C) $\frac{1}{3}$
- (D) $\frac{1}{8}$

10. $56 - 18 \times 2 \div 4 =$
- (F) 19
- (G) 16
- (H) 5
- (J) 47

GO ON

MATH: PRACTICE TEST
Part 2: Computation (cont.)

11. $\frac{3}{4} \div \frac{5}{8} =$

(A) $1\frac{1}{5}$

(B) 2

(C) $\frac{3}{4}$

(D) $1\frac{1}{8}$

12. **23.4 is 30% of what number?**

(F) 68

(G) 140

(H) 88

(J) 78

13. $(86 - 79)(8 \div 7) =$

(A) 12

(B) 9.6

(C) 8.0

(D) 81

14. $\frac{^-96}{^-12}$

(F) 8

(G) $^-8$

(H) $^-18$

(J) 18

15. $\frac{17}{20}$
$\frac{13}{20}$
$+ $

(A) 11

(B) $1\frac{1}{2}$

(C) 101

(D) none of these

16. $3\frac{1}{8} \times \frac{3}{7} =$

(F) $2\frac{15}{56}$

(G) $3\frac{1}{5}$

(H) $4\frac{1}{28}$

(J) none of these

17. $\frac{(95 + 5) - 10}{5}$

(A) 18

(B) 85

(C) 10

(D) none of these

18. $^-43 + ^-9 =$

(F) 34

(G) $^-52$

(H) $^-34$

(J) 52

19. $\frac{9}{10} \times \frac{14}{100} =$

(A) 0.126

(B) 0.0126

(C) 0.8116

(D) 0.08116

20. $6.216 \overline{)803.7288}$

(F) 1.293

(G) 12.93

(H) 129.3

(J) 1293

21. $6\frac{2}{3} + 8\frac{5}{6} =$

(A) $17\frac{1}{2}$

(B) $21\frac{2}{3}$

(C) 24

(D) none of these

22. $(16.3 + 0.027) \div 5.21 =$

(F) 3.323

(G) 3.186

(H) 3.147

(J) 3.134

STOP

Name _____   Date_____

MATH: PRACTICE TEST

● Part 3: Applications

Directions: Read and work each problem. Fill in the circle that corresponds to your choice.

Examples

A. If $2x - 12 = 14$, then $x =$
- Ⓐ 4
- Ⓑ 26
- Ⓒ 16
- Ⓓ 13

B. Molly had a gallon of milk. If she drank a pint, how many cups of milk were left in the container?
- Ⓕ 4 cups
- Ⓖ 3 cups
- Ⓗ 6 cups
- Ⓙ 14 cups

---

1. There are 24 windows in a house. Each window has 2 panes of glass. If it takes 3 minutes to clean one pane, how long will it take to clean all the windows?
- Ⓐ 98 minutes
- Ⓑ 2 hrs. 24 minutes
- Ⓒ 72 minutes
- Ⓓ 1 hour

2. Reba has $750.00 in her bank account. The account earns 3% interest a year. Which equation will tell us how much money will be in the savings account at the end of the year?
- Ⓕ 750 x .03 =
- Ⓖ 750 + (750 x .03) =
- Ⓗ 750 ÷ (.03 x 750) =
- Ⓙ 750 x .03 + .04 =

3. The gas tank in a car holds 22 gallons. It is now half full. If gas costs $1.39 a gallon, which equation will tell us how much will it cost to fill the tank?
- Ⓐ $22 \times \frac{1}{2} + 1.39 =$
- Ⓑ $1.39 \times (22 \times \frac{1}{2}) =$
- Ⓒ $1.39 \times (22 + \frac{1}{2}) =$
- Ⓓ none of the above

4. What is the median of the following set of numbers? **(4, 2, 3, 3, 3, 6)**
- Ⓕ 2
- Ⓖ 3
- Ⓗ 4
- Ⓙ 3.5

5. For which of these equations would $a = 9$ when $b = 6$?
- Ⓐ $3a - 21 = b$
- Ⓑ $2b - a = {}^{-}4$
- Ⓒ $2a - 9 = b$
- Ⓓ $4a - 2b = 18$

6. 12.3 liters is the same as—
- Ⓕ 123 milliliters
- Ⓖ 12.3 milliliters
- Ⓗ 12,300 milliliters
- Ⓙ 1,230 milliliters

7. What is the area of the region shaded below?
- Ⓐ 9.42 ft.²
- Ⓑ 4.54 ft.²
- Ⓒ 3.192 ft.²
- Ⓓ 2.43 ft.²

8. The two soft drink bottles are—

- (F) neither congruent nor similar.
- (G) congruent but not similar.
- (H) similar but not congruent.
- (J) similar and congruent.

9. You take out a loan for $200 with an annual interest rate of 10%. If you make no payments, how long would it take to acquire $66.20 in interest?

- (A) $2\frac{1}{2}$ yrs.
- (B) 2 yrs.
- (C) 3 yrs.
- (D) 4 yrs.

10. You flip a coin 150 times. What is the probability of getting tails on any one flip?

- (F) 1 in 3
- (G) 1 in 2
- (H) 1 in 4
- (J) 1 in 10

11. A sheet of copy paper measures about—

- (A) 3 in. by 4 in.
- (B) 4 in. by 8 in.
- (C) 8 in. by 11 in.
- (D) 12 in. by 16 in.

12. In the triangle below, angle ABC is a right angle. If angle BAC equals 60°, what is the measure of angle ACB?

- (F) 30°
- (G) 45°
- (H) 60°
- (J) 90°

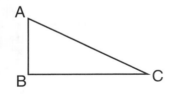

13. What is the total interest earned?

principal	annual rate	time	interest
$100.00	7%	3 years	

- (A) $21.00
- (B) $22.50
- (C) $31.00
- (D) $32.50

14. What fraction of 6 gallons is 6 pints?

- (F) $\frac{1}{48}$
- (G) $\frac{1}{8}$
- (H) $\frac{3}{16}$
- (J) none of these

15. For which of these equations would $a = 5$ when $b = 3$?

- (A) $ab = 12$
- (B) $a^2 = b^2 + 3$
- (C) $2a + b = 13$
- (D) $3a = b + 2$

16. At a family reunion in the Southwest, there were 24 people from California, 18 from New Mexico, and 8 from Arizona. If you began speaking to 1 of the people without knowing where the person was from, what are the chances the person would be from California?

- (F) 1 out of 2
- (G) 24 out of 26
- (H) 12 out of 25
- (J) none of the above

STOP

READING: VOCABULARY
Lesson 1: Synonyms
• Page 7
- A. A
- B. G
- 1. C
- 2. J
- 3. C
- 4. H
- 5. B
- 6. J
- 7. A
- 8. H

Lesson 2: Antonyms
• Page 8
- A. A
- B. G
- 1. D
- 2. H
- 3. D
- 4. H
- 5. A
- 6. H
- 7. D
- 8. G

Lesson 3: Multi-Meaning Words
• Page 9
- A. A
- B. H
- 1. D
- 2. G
- 3. A
- 4. G
- 5. D
- 6. H

Lesson 4: Words in Context
• Page 10
- A. B
- B. F
- 1. C
- 2. H
- 3. D
- 4. F
- 5. B
- 6. J

Lesson 5: Words From Greek and Latin
• Page 11
- A. B
- 1. C
- 2. F
- 3. B
- 4. F
- 5. D
- 6. H

Lesson 6: Shades of Meaning
• Pages 12–13
- A. B
- B. F
- 1. D
- 2. H
- 3. B
- 4. F
- 5. A
- 6. G
- 7. C
- 8. H
- 9. C

- 10. J
- 11. B

Sample Test
• Pages 14–15
- A. C
- B. F
- 1. C
- 2. H
- 3. C
- 4. F
- 5. B
- 6. J
- 7. B
- 8. G
- 9. B
- 10. F
- 11. B
- 12. J
- 13. B
- 14. F
- 15. D
- 16. G
- 17. C
- 18. F

READING: COMPREHENSION
Lesson 7: Main Idea
• Page 16
- A. C
- 1. B
- 2. G
- 3. A

Lesson 8: Recalling Details
• Page 17
- A. B
- 1. B
- 2. F
- 3. C

Lesson 9: Inferences
• Page 18
- A. A
- 1. C
- 2. G

Lesson 10: Fact and Opinion/Drawing Conclusions
• Page 19
- A. C
- 1. D

Lesson 11: Nonfiction
• Pages 20–21
- A. C
- 1. D
- 2. H
- 3. A
- 4. F
- 5. A
- 6. G
- 7. C

Lesson 12: Nonfiction
• Pages 22–23
- A. B
- 1. B
- 2. H
- 3. A
- 4. J
- 5. C
- 6. G

Lesson 13: Nonfiction
• Pages 24–25
- A. A
- 1. C
- 2. G
- 3. C
- 4. G
- 5. D
- 6. F
- 7. B

Lesson 14: Reading Informational Text
• Pages 26–28
- 1. A
- 2. G
- 3. D
- 4. G
- 5. A
- 6. H
- 7. D
- 8. F
- 9. D
- 10. H

Lesson 15: Story Elements
• Page 29
- A. B
- 1. C
- 2. G
- 3. D

Lesson 16: Fiction
• Pages 30–31
- A. C
- 1. A
- 2. J
- 3. A
- 4. F
- 5. C
- 6. G
- 7. A

Lesson 17: Fiction
• Pages 32–33
- A. B
- 1. C
- 2. J
- 3. A
- 4. J
- 5. C
- 6. J
- 7. D

Lesson 18: Fiction
• Pages 34–35
- A. B
- 1. C
- 2. F
- 3. B
- 4. J
- 5. A
- 6. J
- 7. C

Lesson 19: Reading Literature
• Pages 36–38
- 1. B
- 2. F
- 3. A
- 4. J
- 5. B
- 6. H

ANSWER KEY

7. A
8. G
9. D
10. H

Sample Test
• Pages 39–43
A. D
1. A
2. H
3. B
4. F
5. D
6. G
7. B
8. J
9. A
10. H
11. A
12. G
13. D
14. G
15. C
16. J

READING: PRACTICE TEST
Part 1: Vocabulary
• Pages 44–47
A. C
B. F
1. C
2. H
3. A
4. G
5. D
6. F
7. B
8. G
9. D
10. F
11. A
12. G
13. D
14. F
15. B
16. J
17. B
18. H
19. A
20. J
21. B
22. J
23. A
24. G
25. A
26. J
27. C
28. H
29. D
30. G
31. B
32. H

Part 2: Comprehension
• Pages 48–51
A. B
1. D
2. H
3. B
4. F
5. D
6. H

7. A
8. G
9. B
10. F
11. D
12. G
13. B
14. H

LANGUAGE: MECHANICS
Lesson 1: Punctuation
• Pages 52–53
A. D
B. H
1. D
2. F
3. B
4. J
5. B
6. F
7. D
8. F
9. A
10. J
11. C
12. J
13. C
14. H
15. B
16. F
17. B

Lesson 2: Pauses and Omissions
• Page 54
A. D
B. F
1. A
2. H
3. C

Lesson 3: Capitalization and Punctuation
• Pages 55–57
A. A
B. J
1. C
2. J
3. C
4. J
5. A
6. J
7. C
8. F
9. C
10. F
11. B
12. F
13. D
14. H
15. A
16. F
17. C
18. F
19. A
20. F
21. A
22. F
23. D
24. F

Sample Test
• Pages 58–59
A. C
1. D
2. F
3. A
4. H
5. A
6. F
7. C
8. F
9. C
10. H
11. D
12. F
13. D
14. J
15. A

LANGUAGE: EXPRESSION
Lesson 4: Usage
• Pages 60–62
A. D
B. G
1. B
2. H
3. A
4. F
5. D
6. G
7. D
8. G
9. A
10. H
11. A
12. J
13. D
14. F
15. D
16. H
17. D
18. G
19. D
20. H

Lesson 5: Using Verbs
• Pages 63–64
A. A
B. G
1. C
2. J
3. C
4. G
5. A
6. J
7. A
8. F
9. C
10. H

Lesson 6: Verbals
• Page 65
A. B
1. D
2. H
3. D
4. H
5. B
6. J

Lesson 7: Sentences
• Pages 66–68

A. A
B. F
1. A
2. F
3. B
4. H
5. C
6. G
7. C
8. H
9. C
10. G
11. A
12. F
13. A
14. G
15. D

Lesson 8: Paragraphs
• Pages 69–72

A. B
1. D
2. G
3. D
4. F
5. B
6. H
7. B
8. J
9. A
10. H
11. B
12. F
13. B
14. J

Sample Test
• Pages 73–76

A. B
1. C
2. G
3. D
4. J
5. B
6. G
7. B
8. G
9. B
10. G
11. A
12. J
13. D
14. H
15. C
16. F
17. A
18. J
19. D
20. J

LANGUAGE: SPELLING
Lesson 9: Spelling Skills
• Pages 77–78

A. B
B. G
1. C
2. J

3. D
4. H
5. C
6. F
7. D
8. G
9. D
10. F
11. A
12. J
13. D
14. J
15. B
16. F
17. C

Sample Test
• Pages 79–80

A. C
B. H
1. A
2. H
3. B
4. G
5. D
6. J
7. C
8. H
9. A
10. J
11. B
12. F
13. D
14. G
15. C
16. H
17. A
18. J
19. D

LANGUAGE: STUDY SKILLS
Lesson 10: Study Skills
• Pages 81–83

A. C
1. C
2. G
3. D
4. F
5. A
6. G
7. C
8. H
9. A
10. G
11. C
12. J
13. A
14. H
15. B
16. F
17. D
18. F
19. A
20. G

Sample Test
• Pages 84–86

A. C
B. H
1. D
2. F

3. B
4. G
5. C
6. G
7. A
8. H
9. C
10. H
11. A
12. H
13. C
14. J
15. C
16. H
17. C
18. G

LANGUAGE: PRACTICE TEST
Part 1: Mechanics
• Pages 89–91

A. C
1. C
2. J
3. B
4. G
5. B
6. G
7. D
8. H
9. C
10. G
11. D
12. H
13. A
14. J
15. C
16. H
17. A
18. G
19. B
20. G
21. C

Part 2: Expression
• Pages 92–94

A. D
1. D
2. J
3. D
4. G
5. D
6. G
7. C
8. H
9. A
10. H
11. A
12. F
13. B
14. J
15. D
16. G

Part 3: Spelling
• Pages 95–96

A. C
B. F
1. A
2. H
3. C
4. G

7. A
8. F
9. D
10. H
11. D
12. H
13. C
14. F
15. B
16. J
17. B
18. J
19. B

Part 4: Study Skills
• Pages 97–98
A. C
1. C
2. H
3. B
4. J
5. C
6. H
7. C
8. J
9. C
10. H

MATH: CONCEPTS
Lesson 1: Numeration
• Pages 99–101
A. B
B. J
1. B
2. F
3. D
4. G
5. B
6. G
7. D
8. G
9. B
10. F
11. D
12. F
13. B
14. H
15. B
16. H
17. C
18. G
19. B
20. H
21. C
22. G
23. C
24. H

Lesson 2: Number Concepts
• Pages 102–104
A. C
B. F
1. B
2. H
3. C
4. F
5. B
6. H
7. B
8. H
9. D

10. F
11. C
12. J
13. D
14. H
15. C
16. G
17. B
18. F
19. A
20. J
21. C

Lesson 3: Rational and Irrational Numbers
• Page 105
A. B
B. H
1. C
2. G
3. B
4. F
5. B

Lesson 4: Scientific Notation
• Page 106
A. D
B. H
1. B
2. H
3. B
4. H
5. A

Lesson 5: Fractions and Decimals
• Pages 107–109
A. D
B. F
1. B
2. F
3. B
4. H
5. D
6. J
7. C
8. J
9. B
10. G
11. A
12. F
13. D
14. H
15. C
16. H
17. A
18. J
19. B
20. J
21. D
22. H

Lesson 6: Proportional Relationships
• Page 110
A. C
1. B
2. H

Sample Test
• Pages 111–113
A. A
B. G
1. C

2. H
3. C
4. J
5. D
6. J
7. C
8. H
9. C
10. H
11. B
12. H
13. B
14. G
15. B
16. F
17. C
18. G
19. D
20. G
21. B
22. F
23. C
24. J

MATH: COMPUTATION
Lesson 7: Whole Numbers
• Pages 114–115
A. B
B. C
1. C
2. F
3. D
4. G
5. B
6. F
7. D
8. G
9. A
10. J
11. B
12. F
13. C
14. G
15. B
16. F
17. C

Lesson 8: Decimals
• Pages 116–117
A. C
B. J
1. B
2. F
3. D
4. F
5. C
6. F
7. B
8. H
9. C
10. G
11. D
12. G
13. A
14. F
15. A
16. F
17. A

Lesson 9: Percent

• Pages 118–119
- A. B
- B. G
- 1. A
- 2. G
- 3. D
- 4. F
- 5. C
- 6. H
- 7. B
- 8. G
- 9. C
- 10. G
- 11. A
- 12. H
- 13. C
- 14. H
- 15. A
- 16. H
- 17. B

Lesson 10: Fractions
• Pages 120–121
- A. C
- B. F
- 1. C
- 2. F
- 3. A
- 4. H
- 5. D
- 6. J
- 7. B
- 8. G
- 9. B
- 10. H
- 11. A
- 12. H
- 13. C
- 14. F
- 15. D
- 16. G

Sample Test
• Pages 122–124
- A. D
- B. F
- 1. A
- 2. G
- 3. B
- 4. H
- 5. B
- 6. G
- 7. D
- 8. F
- 9. A
- 10. J
- 11. D
- 12. H
- 13. D
- 14. G
- 15. C
- 16. G
- 17. A
- 18. G
- 19. C
- 20. F
- 21. D
- 22. F
- 23. C
- 24. G

MATH: APPLICATIONS
Lesson 11: Geometry
• Pages 125–127
- A. C
- 1. C
- 2. H
- 3. B
- 4. H
- 5. B
- 6. G
- 7. D
- 8. J
- 9. B
- 10. H
- 11. D
- 12. H
- 13. A
- 14. H
- 15. A
- 16. G

Lesson 12: Congruence and Similarity
• Pages 128–129
- A. D
- B. F
- 1. B
- 2. H
- 3. A
- 4. H
- 5. B

Lesson 13: The Pythagorean Theorem
• Page 130
- A. B
- B. H
- 1. D
- 2. H
- 3. C
- 4. G
- 5. C

Lesson 14: Measurement
• Pages 131–132
- A. A
- 1. C
- 2. G
- 3. B
- 4. H
- 5. C
- 6. H
- 7. B
- 8. H
- 9. A
- 10. G
- 11. B
- 12. H
- 13. C
- 14. G
- 15. A

Lesson 15: Volume
• Page 133
- A. C
- B. F
- 1. B
- 2. G
- 3. C
- 4. H
- 5. A

Lesson 16: Problem Solving
• Pages 134–136
- A. B
- B. G
- 1. B
- 2. G
- 3. D
- 4. G
- 5. C
- 6. G
- 7. A
- 8. H
- 9. D
- 10. H
- 11. B
- 12. J
- 13. C
- 14. F
- 15. B
- 16. J

Lesson 17: Algebra
• Pages 137–138
- A. D
- B. F
- 1. B
- 2. J
- 3. D
- 4. G
- 5. C
- 6. G
- 7. D
- 8. H
- 9. A
- 10. G
- 11. B
- 12. H

Lesson 18: Linear Equations
• Page 139
- A. C
- B. H
- 1. C
- 2. J
- 3. D
- 4. J

Lesson 19: Functions
• Pages 140–142
- A. A
- 1. C
- 2. G
- 3. A
- 4. F
- 5. A
- 6. H
- 7. D
- 8. H
- 9. B
- 10. J
- 11. C
- 12. G
- 13. A

Lesson 20: Patterns in Data
• Pages 143–144
- 1. C
- 2. F
- 3. D
- 4. H
- 5. B
- 6. H

7. B
8. H
9. C
10. J

Sample Test
• Pages 145–148
A. B
B. G
1. C
2. J
3. D
4. G
5. C
6. G
7. B
8. G
9. C
10. F
11. B
12. H
13. D
14. H
15. D
16. F
17. C
18. G
19. C
20. G
21. C
22. J
23. B
24. F
25. C
26. G

MATH: PRACTICE TEST
Part 1: Concepts
• Pages 149–150
A. A
B. J
1. C
2. G
3. A
4. H
5. C
6. F
7. B
8. G
9. C
10. J
11. B
12. G
13. A
14. J
15. C
16. J
17. B

Part 2: Computation
• Pages 151–152
A. C
B. F
1. B
2. F
3. C
4. H
5. B
6. J
7. C
8. H

9. B
10. J
11. A
12. J
13. C
14. F
15. B
16. J
17. A
18. G
19. A
20. H
21. D
22. J

Part 3: Applications
• Pages 153–154
A. D
B. J
1. B
2. G
3. B
4. G
5. A
6. H
7. A
8. H
9. C
10. G
11. C
12. F
13. B
14. G
15. C
16. H